Software Shock

Software Shock
The Danger & The Opportunity

by Roger S. Pressman
and S. Russell Herron

Dorset House Publishing
353 West 12th Street
New York, New York 10014

Library of Congress Cataloging in Publication Data

Pressman, Roger S.
    Software shock : the danger & the opportunity / by Roger S.
Pressman and S. Russell Herron.
        p.   cm.
    Includes bibliographical references and index.
    ISBN 0-932633-20-X
    1. Computer software. 2. Computer software industry.   I. Herron
S. Russell. 1944-   . II. Title.
QA76.754.P74   1991
338.4'70053--dc20   91-20988
                                                CIP

Authors' Note: The vignettes in this book are all based on real circumstances and conversations, but we have used fictitious names to maintain the privacy of our clients and colleagues.

Pen and ink illustrations for the cover and the chapter openings by Ron Logan. Copyright © 1991 by Ron Logan.

Cover type design by Jeff Faville, Faville Graphics

Copyright © 1991 by Roger S. Pressman and S. Russell Herron. Published by Dorset House Publishing, 353 West 12th Street, New York, NY 10014.

Distributed in the United Kingdom, Ireland, Europe, and Africa by John Wiley & Sons Ltd., Chichester, Sussex, England.

Printed in the United States of America

Library of Congress Catalog Number 91-20988
ISBN: 0-932633-20-X   12 11 10 9 8 7 6 5 4 3 2 1

Contents

Acknowledgments

We each have spent more than twenty years in the software business. Over the years, hundreds of managers, customers, programmers, engineers, and innocent computer users have paraded through our careers and affected our perception of the software business. We've learned invaluable lessons about computing and about life from many of them. Many are presented within the pages of this book. To all, our thanks.

Special thanks to Gene Forte whose insight, suggestions, and criticism did much to help us improve the original manuscript; the many reviewers, whose comments helped us to focus our thoughts; and Janice Wormington, whose editorial guidance helped us to polish the final product.

Finally, we'd like to express our love and thanks to Barbara and Sherry, who not only provided us with support throughout this effort, but also did everything possible to keep us from writing in computerese.

Preface

Have you ever wondered where software comes from and where it's going, why computer programs don't always work, who builds them, and how they do it? Have you ever thought about what a software product really is, or why companies often spend enormous amounts of money building computer programs? Have you ever encountered people who become disoriented and stressed when asked to use computers and software, and others who are intrigued and drawn to the technology? If you have, *Software Shock* has been written for you.

If you don't know much about computers and software, we hope to make you a little bit smarter. If you're a person who uses computers, we'll try to broaden your understanding. If you're a professional person or a manager, we'll explain some of software's dangers and many of its opportunities. We've written *Software Shock* for anyone who'd like to learn more about software—the engine that drives every computer.

Although we've written this book in a light, anecdotal style, there is an underlying seriousness to its content. Unless far more people understand the importance of software to our society—both the opportunities as well as the dangers—we may be heading for a crisis—a time when faulty software causes serious economic and even human damage; and a time when it prevents our advance in other critical technological areas.

We don't suggest that this book will save us from a software crisis. We do believe that understanding a technology is the first step toward controlling it, and *Software Shock* will help you to understand.

April 1991

Roger S. Pressman
Orange, Connecticut

S. Russell Herron
Houston, Texas

Credits

Our thanks for use of the following excerpts:

In Chapter 2, from E.W. Dijkstra, "On the Cruelty of Really Teaching Computing Science," *Communications of the ACM*, Vol. 32, No. 12 (December 1989), p. 1398. Copyright © 1989. Reprinted by permission of the publisher.

In Chapter 3, from Peter Mellor, "Risks to the Public in Computers and Related Systems," P.G. Neumann, moderator. *ACM Sigsoft Notes*, Vol. 15, No. 5 (October 1990), p. 14. Copyright © 1990. Reprinted by permission.

In Part III, from Gail Sheehy, *Passages: Predictable Crises of Adult Life* (New York: E.P. Dutton, 1976), p. 11. Copyright © 1976. Reprinted by permission of the publisher.

In Chapter 6, from Steven Levy, *Hackers: Heroes of the Computer Revolution* (Garden City, N.Y.: Anchor Press/Doubleday, 1984), p. 1. Copyright © 1984. Reprinted by permission of the publisher.

In Chapter 7, from G.J. Myers, *Composite/Structured Design* (New York: Van Nostrand Reinhold, 1978), p. 2. Copyright © 1978. Reprinted by permission of the publisher.

In Chapter 7, from T.J. Peters and R.H. Waterman, Jr., *In Search of Excellence* (New York: Harper & Row, 1982), p. 157. Copyright © 1982. Reprinted by permission of the publisher.

In Chapter 7, from T. DeMarco and T. Lister, *Peopleware* (New York: Dorset House Publishing, 1987), p. 123. Copyright © 1987. Reprinted by permission of the publisher.

In Chapter 8, from R. Pirsig, *Zen and the Art of Motorcycle Maintenance* (New York: William Morrow & Co., 1974), pp. 228-29, 237. Copyright © 1974 by Robert M. Pirsig. Reprinted by permission of the publisher.

In Chapter 8, from P. Crosby, *Quality Is Free* (New York: McGraw-Hill, 1979), pp. 13-14. Copyright © 1979. In Chapter 10, from Roger Pressman, *Software Engineering: A Practitioner's Approach*, 3rd ed. (New York: McGraw-Hill, 1992). Copyright © 1992, 1987, 1982. Reprinted by permission.

In Chapter 1, from F.P. Brooks, Jr., *The Mythical Man-Month* (Reading, Mass.: Addison-Wesley, 1975), p. 177. Copyright © 1975. In Chapter 5, from E.A. Feigenbaum and P. McCorduck, *The Fifth Generation* (Reading, Mass.: Addison-Wesley, 1983), p. 1. Copyright © 1983. In Chapter 7, from B. Shneiderman, *Designing the User Interface* (Reading, Mass.: Addison-Wesley, 1987), p. *v*. Copyright © 1987. Reprinted by permission of the publisher.

Software Shock

The Roller Coaster

Introduction:
The Invisible Revolution

"What line of work are you in?" asks a garrulous cabby as he whisks me (RSP) through heavy traffic to make an appointment.

"Software—you know, computers."

"Oh, yeah, computers. Boy, it seems like everyone's into computers," he says. "What do you do, build 'em or sell 'em?"

"Well, neither, I show people the best ways to program them."

The cabby ponders this for a moment, taking time out to curse a delivery truck that has cut him off. "Oh, programming. Don't understand it, but I hear some of my fares talk about it.

"Don't get involved with computers myself," the cabby muses. "Way I look at it, computers are a pain in the neck. The only time I even notice one is when it screws up my paycheck."

The meter that he used was computerized. His cab couldn't move without its computerized fuel injection system. The traffic lights that he ran were synchronized by computer; the dazzling effects on the electronic billboards along his route were displayed by computer; the location of every cab was tracked by computer. The cabby's involvement with computers—with software—was continuous. Yet, he didn't realize it.

The cabby and many like him are now so accustomed to the impact of computing that it has become part of the background noise of life in the 1990s. Although we're vaguely aware of its presence, we often don't pay much attention. It has become invisible.

We are in the midst of a technological revolution . . . a revolution so profound no one in our society will be untouched. The spark that ignited the revolution was a machine—the computer—but the flame that keeps the revolution burning is something with less physical substance and far more importance: computer software.

Software is a means for automating business, industry, and government. It is a medium for transferring new technology, a method of capturing knowledge so that it can be used by others, a way to differentiate one company's products from its competitors, and a window into a corporation's decision making processes. It is pivotal to nearly every aspect of business and is a business in and of itself.

Although software touches everyone's life, it is a hidden technology. We encounter software (often without realizing it) when we travel to work, buy groceries, stop at the bank, make a phone call, visit the doctor, or perform any of the hundreds of daily activities of modern life. We notice its effects without seeing it. We use it without knowing it is there. We become aware of it only when something goes awry and, even then, we may blame the wrong thing.

On the surface, software is a rather simple technology. It is the programs that cause a computer to perform some function. Through software, we control the computer. And in a way, the computer controls us. But there is also an emotional and very human component to software. When we use it, it changes us. We enter new worlds of complex systems, of new information and new insights and new experiences.

When we experience this new technology, some of us adapt rapidly, while others of us do not. We may become stressed and disoriented, or apathetic, or hostile to the changes being made. We may suffer *software shock*—a feeling of powerlessness and confusion and of being out of control.

In his landmark book on rapid technological change, Alvin Toffler coined the term *future shock* "to describe the shattering stress and disorientation that we induce in individuals by subjecting them to too much change in too short a time."* We encounter a similar phenomenon as our governments, businesses, and personal lives become intertwined with computer systems and the software that drives them. When these systems work, the results are often so good we experience a euphoric sense of control. Trends are obvious, response is instantaneous, information is readily available, and products are customized to meet particular needs.

But when software and its systems or products fail or when we become overwhelmed by interacting with a computer system, we encounter *software shock*—the stress and disorientation induced in individuals and groups when software controls our work, home, products, toys, government, and even our entertainment. Software shock can affect all of us—software professionals, business managers, nontechnical professionals, blue collar workers—everyone who must build, buy, sell, or use products, systems, or services that contain software.

The symptoms of software shock vary. Some people become technophobic, avoiding computer-based technologies at all cost. Some become Luddites, sabotaging even good systems in an effort to go back to the old ways. Some become angry, demanding proof that software is better than previous methods for information generation, storage, and control. Some become unreasonable, expecting too much in too short a time, and then complaining when these unreasonable demands can't be met.

Are we approaching a crisis—a time when companies lose revenue because their products containing software don't work, a time when managers lack critical business data because the program to produce the data is grievously behind schedule, a time when air travel is canceled because the air traffic control system cannot handle the traffic load, a time when systems that work all too well intrude on our privacy, jeopardize our safety, or complicate our world? It is

---

*A. Toffler, *Future Shock* (New York: Bantam Books, 1970), p. 2.

at times like these that the impact of software can reach crisis proportions.

A language from a civilization much older than ours provides insight into the true meaning of a software crisis. The Japanese word for *crisis* is is made up of two Kanji characters: The first character means *danger;* the second character means *hidden opportunity.* Interestingly, a software crisis can represent danger for those who disregard it, and opportunity for those who take advantage of it.

Toffler summarizes the situation nicely: "Given a clearer grasp of the problems and more intelligent control of certain key processes, we can turn crisis into opportunity, helping people not merely to survive, but to crest the waves of change, to grow and to gain a new sense of mastery over their own destinies."*

About This Book

We have organized this book into four parts, each written to help you in your journey toward understanding software technology. Through understanding, you'll be better able to avoid the dangers and exploit the opportunities.

A successful journey demands that the traveler know two facts: where you are and where you're going. Part I addresses where software is today, and where it is heading over the next few decades.

Like any technology, software is much more than dry technical principles, theories, and rules. People are involved from the moment software is conceived until the day it is retired from use. People create it, sell it, buy it, and use it and through their activities create cultures that are as colorful as they are varied. Part II introduces the cultures, people, and technology of the software industry, and puts them into a historical context. The chapters in this part offer a brief glimpse of the early days of computing and examine their legacy for today's technologists.

---

*Ibid., p. 374.

In Part III, we explore the people involved and their roles in more detail, the cultures they form, and the interactions that result.

Travel always broadens the traveler. You learn from the people you meet and the things you see. You remember the experience and apply what you've learned at journey's end. Part IV discusses how to make software technology work for you, regardless of your profession or level of technical skill.

As we journey together, you will read facts that will broaden your knowledge and vignettes that will solidify your understanding. Although each is a small detour, all collectively add to the experience. Bon voyage!

Part I
Today and Tomorrow

Palo Alto, California

A small child is brought into a hospital complaining of severe headaches. After a preliminary exam, the physician decides he needs more information.

"We'll need a CAT scan," he says to a nurse. "Call Dr. Miller. I'll need a consult." Miller is a radiologist. His diagnostic instruments include a powerful computer graphics workstation that is electronically networked to the radiology lab. Information from the CAT scan will be transmitted to Miller's office. The information is processed, and two- or three-dimensional color images of the child's brain are displayed for the physician.

Examining the CAT scan, Miller has a feeling of déjà vu, but can't place what he's seeing. He turns to the computerized database and retrieves past cases with similar characteristics; he overlays the images and subtracts the differences graphically. Surrounded by hardware, Miller continues his diagnosis. But the technology that helps his diagnosis is not the powerful workstation or the computer graphics or the wires inside the CAT scanner. It's something else.

London, England

Heels click on the polished marble floors and echo along a teak-paneled hallway of one of the world's largest international banks. Three floors above, a different ambience awaits.

Claire Worthington is a currency trader. Her tools are her knowledge, experience, and a computer workstation linking her with hundreds of financial institutions worldwide. Through four windows on the workstation screen, she watches transactions in the money markets that she tracks. As the windows simultaneously flash price quotes, spreadsheets, graphs, and messages, she makes trades, sends messages, and gets advice.

As Worthington scans the windows, she sees an unusual pattern of trading. She hits a few keys and invokes an expert system to analyze the trades and recommend action. But the expert system suggests actions that make little sense. She enters the data again, and her keystrokes result in the same odd instructions. Should she follow the suggestions of the machine, or do nothing?

"Damn this computer," the trader yells, as she lunges for the telephone. Claire Worthington is blaming a machine—she should be blaming something else.

Benito Juarez International Airport, Mexico City, Mexico

A jumbo jet taxis toward runway one south for a scheduled trip to Buenos Aires. The flight crew goes through the boring but necessary ritual of pre-flight checks. Co-captain José Dieguez grabs the cabin phone, flicks the broadcast button, and begins his "Welcome on board. Flight attendants prepare the aircraft" speech.

The jet lumbers down the runway and, almost a mile later, lifts off the ground. But at an altitude of a hundred meters, there is a loud pop and black smoke pours out of an engine. Before the passengers realize what's happening, the aircraft pitches badly to one side. As the crew starts to react, the plane rights itself. After a minute, Dieguez is back on the cabin phone reassuring the passengers about the small problem that will require a return to the airport for repair.

Upon landing, more than one relieved passenger thanks the crew for avoiding a disaster. The crew should be thanked, but the passengers don't realize that something else was also involved.

Different people, different places, different situations, but all with a common thread. Yes, computers were involved in every scenario, but the computers were merely a delivery vehicle for the technology that really mattered. The technology is software.

In the chapters that follow, we'll examine software for what it is today and for what it may become tomorrow.

The Towers

I

Hackers, Headaches, and Headlines

Someone once remarked that a technology that is sufficiently far advanced is indistinguishable from magic. For many people, software technology is sufficiently far advanced. Amazed and sometimes frightened by what they see, these people are oblivious to the potential impact of the technology. Is it good magic or bad magic? They don't have a clue.

In the heady first days of computing, generally regarded as the 1950s, a few technologists and most of the media couldn't resist talking about "thinking machines." With its electronic "brain," computers could "think" faster than humans, and so many believed they would soon be able to think better. The truth was a bit more mundane.

Colin Pettenridge, an English scientist who began working with computing machines during this era, called the computer "the most significant of human inventions because it complements the human brain in precisely the two ways which limit the brain—slowness and boredom." A cynical viewpoint, no doubt, but reasonably close to the mark.

Since then, the popular press has made often futile attempts to explain how this "most significant of human inventions" worked. Try as they might, the media couldn't capture the essence of computers because the essence isn't metal, or plastic, or blinking lights, or wires, or circuits. The essence of a computer is the programs— the *software* that gives the machine its worth.

Software: Process and Product

Just what is software? Is it simply a magnetic diskette encased in plastic fed into the front of a computer? Or is it something more? Throughout this book, we'll be talking about software, so we need to establish a working definition:

Software is the information used to tap the potential of a computer.

Software is actually an information composite: It is information, it uses information, and it creates information. That's what makes it so difficult to understand, and that's also what makes it so powerful. Software is the computer programs that control the electronic hardware and perform processing tasks for the user; it is the external manifestation of those programs seen by the computer user; it is the documents that describe how the programs work and how they are to be used; and, finally, it is the data that are used by the programs as well as the data that are produced by them.

To make matters worse, software can refer to both the *product* as well as the *process*. The product, as we've said, manifests itself in many ways—from bank teller machines to desktop publishing systems. Software as a process encompasses both people and technology and has much to do with both the success and impact of the product.

Computers have undergone dramatic changes since the 1960s. They have become considerably more powerful and dramatically less expensive. But software has not undergone the same degree of change. For the most part, the structure and internal details of a computer program written in 1965 are quite similar to ones written today. Certainly, software applications have become more complex, but software has not changed as radically as the machines on which it is executed. The product has undergone only slow, evolutionary change.

And what of the process? We measure improvements in hardware by factors of ten. We measure improvements in software using a much, much smaller ruler. Over a thirty-year period, hardware has improved at a compound annual rate of approximately twenty-five percent. The software process has improved at a compound annual rate of about four percent. This disparity between hardware and software improvement has been the topic of hundreds of articles, essays, editorials, and speeches in the various technical forums. In the end, almost every discussion comes to the same conclusion: Building software is a people-intensive activity. It is much more difficult to improve a person's performance than it is to improve a machine's efficiency.

Therefore, any discussion of software leads us to the people who create computer programs. Software would not exist without them.

Hackers—A Culture Emerges

Ada Augusta Lovelace was the charter member of a club that today numbers more than one million members in the United States. An English author and science historian in the early to mid-1800s, she worked with Charles Babbage on the analytical engine, the predecessor to the modern computer. Ada, Countess of Lovelace and daughter of the poet Lord Byron, was the world's first computer programmer (the Ada programming language was named for her).

Almost a century and a half passed before membership in the club grew. Herman Goldstine and Julian Bigelow, working at Princeton's Institute of Advanced Studies on an electronic computer designed by John von Neumann, are thought to be the first modern computer programmers. These men and the thousands that have followed in their footsteps chose a profession with an exciting future, but no past. There was little history to study, few traditions to call upon, and no set rules for accomplishing the work. To fill this void, programmers quickly developed their own culture, far different from the engineers and business people with whom they interacted and far removed from others who used the programs they created. They established a language of their own, with jargon that excluded those outside of their culture. They defined traditions to pass along to future generations. They developed and refined skills and branched into areas of specialization.

As the culture established itself, its high priests were given a new name. Sure, they would remain programmers to the outside world, but within their closed community, they became *hackers*. Hackers were knowledgeable, creative, sometimes brilliant programmers who viewed themselves as artists. To the hacker, rules were anathema, and teamwork was evil. Hackers "just did it."

Today, the popular definition of hacker is somewhat different— or is it? The modern-day hacker is the mutant descendant of an earlier culture, someone who breaks into supposedly secure computer systems, stealing information and using it for advantage; someone who creates viruses that ruin other people's work, and then worms those viruses into computer networks; someone who is a knowledgeable, creative, sometimes brilliant programmer who views himself as an artist. Sound familiar? Kent Alexander, an Atlanta District Attorney who prosecutes hackers, characterizes them this way: "I'm convinced that if Lotus 1-2-3 was behind door number 1 and Cheryl Tiegs was standing behind door number 2, a hacker would go for the software."[*]

The hacker's culture flourished during the 1960s and 1970s, and remnants of it still exist today. Yet a new culture is forming. Programmers are more disciplined. They're working on teams, as software projects become increasingly complex. They're using automated tools to improve the quality of the systems they build. And they're using a methodology, as they recognize the ad hoc approach just doesn't work any longer. Programmers are adopting this new culture and, in the process, they are becoming *software engineers*.

Headaches—Quality and Timeliness

During the 1980s, the computer industry advanced at warp speed. Personal computers became almost as common as the telephone; networks linking computers throughout large companies were installed by the hundreds; and embedded computer-based products often had more computing power than a mainframe computer of the 1970s. One computer vendor bragged, "If the auto industry did what the computer industry has done, a Rolls Royce would get a thousand miles to the gallon, go a million miles per hour, and cost $99."

As computing power has increased, companies have spent enormous sums on computers and software. In 1988 alone, companies in the U.S. spent some $50 billion on computer hardware.

---

[*]J.R. Wilke, "In the Arcane Culture of Computer Hackers, Few Doors Stay Closed," *The Wall Street Journal*, August 22, 1990, p. 4a.

In that same year, they spent more than $60 billion on purchased software and computing services.

With each step in technological innovation, the demand for high-quality, timely software increased. In response, software companies proliferated and reached the Fortune 500. Microsoft, Lotus, Oracle, and many others each had annual revenues approaching a half billion dollars. Hundreds of smaller companies also jumped into the software market. The opportunities for growth seemed unbounded and the choices for software products appeared endless.

Some of the demand could be met by off-the-shelf software sold by companies like those mentioned above. Much of the demand, however, was for custom software, programs built to meet a specific business need. Unfortunately, custom software is difficult and expensive to build, and, as we'll see in Chapter 9, it creates major headaches for both the managers who request it as well as the technologists who build it. Often, custom software takes more time to create than originally expected, and it often doesn't work as well as it should. It requires people, money, and time. In today's corporate environment—an environment that demands downsizing, cost reduction, and rapid time to market—people, money, and time are in short supply.

These problems are not difficult to understand, just difficult to fix. How can American industry build software to tap the potential offered by advancing computer technology and still maintain the quality and timeliness of the products, systems, and services that are integrated with this technology? That is the question we'll answer in the coming pages.

Headlines—Out of the Closet and into Our Minds

Beneath the familiar *Business Week* logotype, the two-inch headline caught the eye of even the most casual observer. "Software: The New Driving Force," it proclaimed. The year was 1984 (somehow appropriate), and the headline was the first note in a chorus of newspaper stories and magazine articles about software—a topic once reserved for trade and scientific journals. Software had come out of the closet.

Software headlines have moved from the pages of technical journals to those of the popular press.

It seemed that every article about software told a story with the same plot. It would begin with a labored attempt to describe just what software is ("the instructions that allow the computer to work" or "the codes that the computer follows"). Next, it would describe the wondrous opportunities software promised (all-electronic homes and talking appliances, for example). Then, in proper balance, it would warn of the dangers posed by the technology, as one or more horror stories were related ("Company X loses millions due to programming error" or "Woman receives utility bill for $1,350,000"). Finally, the article would lament the shortage of competent programmers and ask, "How are we to meet the demand?"

In all of these articles, the projections through the year 2000 showed the demand for new programs far exceeding the supply of people available to develop them. In fact, the demand has been projected to increase at an exponential rate. By extrapolation, we'd have to conclude that every man, woman, and child in the U.S. would have to be a computer programmer by 2025 to meet the demand for software. A ridiculous projection? Let's consider it for a moment.

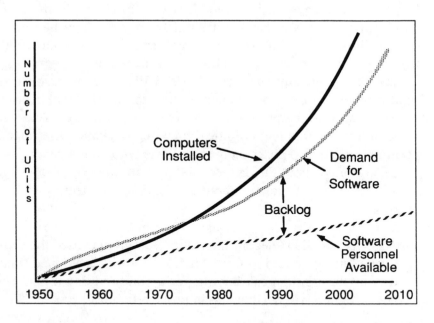

Projections of the growth of computer hardware, software demand, and people to service the demand as a function of time.

In 1920, a new technology captured the imagination of many Americans. It was rapidly shrinking the country; it was becoming a fixture in every house; it was creating new industries. That new technology was the telephone. As the futurists of that day attempted to project the growth of the telephone, they became more and more concerned. In 1920, the telephone switching system was a mostly manual affair, requiring thousands of operators to service even a medium-sized city. Technology writers of the day projected the growth of the telephone and concluded that by 1960, every man, woman, and child would have to be a telephone operator to service the projected demand!

The funny thing is they were right: We all did become "operators," but the technology changed in such a profound fashion that being an operator was much different from what they had envisioned. Similarly, the futurists writing during the 1980s and 1990s may prove to be correct in predicting everyone will be a programmer (time will tell), but software technologies will change in such a profound manner that the programmer or engineer of 2025 will bear little resemblance to the programmer or engineer of today. We are at the beginning of this technological change—a change that offers opportunities but also poses dangers to those who do not adapt.

The stories about the dangers and opportunities are front page news—stories about money, about crime, about amazing new discoveries:

- A newly installed telecommunications program caused the California lottery system to fail. All 4,375 terminals stopped functioning during the peak buying period on Saturday night. The new program was designed to improve reliability.

  —*Los Angeles Times*

- Drawing on the principles of sexual reproduction and Charles Darwin's theory of natural selection, a computer scientist at

Stanford University has patented a method for "breeding" computer programs as if they were tomatoes.

—New York Times

- A computer software error at Wells Fargo Bank resulted in delay in depositing payroll checks for 12,000 to 15,000 workers in 70 companies in Northern California. The bank promised to cover any overdraft charges.

—San Francisco Chronical

- A California computer hacker named Kevin L. Poulsen, code name "Dark Dante," was indicted with a bizarre range of computer crime that included illegally obtaining the phone number of the late Philippine dictator Ferdinand Marcos to eavesdropping on telephone conversations of young women. Most serious was the allegation that Poulsen penetrated an Army computer network and obtained classified information.

—Newsweek

- Xerox Corp.'s Silicon Valley Laboratories envisions a new approach called "ubiquitous computing." An average executive in the mid-1990s would have a dozen note-sized computers (that mimic Post-It Notes®) scattered around the office for quick memos. "We're taking life as it is and computerizing it," says a Xerox research manager.

—Wall Street Journal

- The number of PCs turned salesmen is growing fast. Advertisers spent about $10 million a year on computer disk ads, up from almost nothing three years ago. A handful of "software ad agencies" work on the principle that computer users are the most captive of captive audiences.

—Newsweek

Software is everywhere. It has an impact on just about everything. We live in a world that relies on computers and software.

When things go wrong with software—when it's behind schedule, when it fails and makes us look bad, when it's difficult or frustrating to use, when it's unreliable or unmaintainable—we suffer *software shock*. But even when nothing is wrong—when software is available to meet our needs, when it works well and makes us look good, when it's easy to use, reliable and flexible—we can still suffer the shock that is precipitated by rapid change.

What can happen to those who succumb to software shock is illustrated best by an image chosen by noted computer expert Frederick Brooks. Years ago, in a now classic collection of essays, Brooks chose a line drawing of a prehistoric tar pit, where saber-toothed tigers, mammoths, and great bear-like creatures struggled mightily to extract themselves from the tar. Brooks explains:

> The tar pit of software engineering will continue to be sticky for a long time to come. One can expect the human race to continue attempting systems just within or just beyond our reach; and software systems are perhaps the most intricate and complex of man's handiworks. The management of this complex craft will demand our best use of new languages and systems, our best adaptation of proven engineering management methods, liberal doses of common sense, and a God-given humility to recognize our fallibility and limitations.[*]

The tar pit of software continues to be very sticky indeed. In fact, as software use continues to spread, the pit seems to grow. And people everywhere who were previously untouched may encounter the tar for the first time.

---

[*]F.P. Brooks, Jr., *The Mythical Man-Month* (Reading, Mass.: Addison-Wesley, 1975), p. 177.

But we are not doomed to sink into the tar pit. If we under-stand what software is, if we realize the dangers and appreciate the opportunities, software can be used effectively to benefit us all. In the chapters that follow, we'll show you why.

Runaway

2
Software in the Twenty-first Century

The usual way in which we plan today for tomorrow is in yesterday's vocabulary. . . . By means of metaphors and analogies, we try to link the new to the old, the novel to the familiar. Under sufficiently slow and gradual change, it works reasonably well; in the case of sharp discontinuity, however, the method breaks down.[*]

It is likely there will be "sharp discontinuity" in the growth of computing over the next twenty or thirty years. Yet, this discontinuity is extremely difficult to predict. Therefore (with all due respect to Edsger Dijkstra), we will use metaphor and analogy to suggest our vision of software in the twenty-first century.

---

[*]E.W. Dijkstra, "On the Cruelty of Really Teaching Computing Science," *Communications of the ACM*, Vol. 32, No. 12 (December 1989), p. 1398.

Software is the fuel that will power us into the twenty-first century. It is the power behind intelligent products perceived to be science fiction only a few years ago. It is the propellant for transporting computers into the home and the power behind automated banking services, shopping, entertainment, and information management. It is the energy behind computer-based education.

But software also has a dark side. If improperly designed or inadequately controlled, software can lead to a society in which privacy no longer exists; to situations in which good intentions lead to dire consequences; to a world in which flawed programs can lead to inconvenience or chaos.

When the automobile was invented, most observers realized that travel would be simplified and that a new industry would be born. But few people foresaw an interstate highway system, massive traffic jams, RVs, or the evolution of suburban America. In fact, not a soul predicted that cars would change the mating habits of American teenagers! There was no easy way to trace the technology to a future that we now know as reality.

We face the same problem in predicting the future of computers and software. It is easy to forecast more powerful machines and programs, but what will they truly mean to each of us? How will our culture change because of them?

In this chapter and the next, we'll attempt a little crystal ball gazing. Because computers and software are inextricably tied to one another, the future of one will undoubtedly have an impact on the other. Therefore, our discussion will focus on computing in the next century, and the implications of uniting hardware, software, and people.

The Workplace

> The engineering manager stared into space, as if conjuring the future. "You know," he mused, "the market forces all of us [major computer companies] to build more and more horsepower [more powerful computers]—and

we do it to stay competitive. But I think we're all missing the point.

"How so?" I (RSP) asked.

"Our real job is to make business easy, and to tell you the truth, horsepower alone is not going to do it."

"So what's the answer? Where do your people have to concentrate their energies?"

"Our company culture forces us to focus on hardware, but it's really software that provides the answer to 'easy.' Programs make the hardware easy to use. They make information easy to get. They create happy customers and that causes our business to grow. "

The executive was absolutely correct, but how do we make business easy? In this section, we'll explore software-based systems that may have a profound impact in making the workplace a much easier environment.

On the Shop Floor

Frank Martieri is a repair technician for a large heavy equipment manufacturer. When he started his job twenty years ago, he pushed a rolling tool cart that he called his traveling repair shop. Today, Martieri doesn't use the cart. When a machine fails, he attaches a small diagnostic computer to its side. Soon, this computer displays a code and a location. The code indicates one of eighty different problems, and the location pinpoints the machine subsystem that is in trouble. Martieri then returns to his office and asks the maintenance diagnostic system (via a computer terminal) for a customized repair record for the machine and a detailed listing of actions to fix it.

Frank Martieri is one of millions of low-tech workers who have been transformed into users of high-tech equipment. Interacting with an intelligent machine—whether it's an automated weaving machine, a numerically controlled lathe, a welding robot, or a word processor—takes more skill and demands more analytical decision making. Automation makes machines more flexible, but the workers who interact with them must become more flexible in turn. A recent article on the impact of computing in the workplace agrees:

> Computer technology and automation have taken the sweat and tedium out of many jobs, from coal mining to clerical work. Yet work has become far more complex and mentally demanding. No longer can workers count on performing one task day in and day out. Now they must handle a variety of skills, make snap decisions and adapt to unpredictable changes.*

Computer technology and automation are what we see as we walk through a manufacturing facility, but it is the software that is the catalyst for the profound changes in both the blue collar and white collar workplaces. It is also the software that will make or break acceptance of these changes because software itself determines how easy it will be for people to interact with the automation.

But "ease of use" means more than simple interaction. It also means that the computer programs anticipate the user's needs, guide the user through difficult procedures, protect the user from making an error, and control the impact of any mistake that does slip through.

If programs are unreliable, unadaptable, or incorrect, workplace productivity is reduced—not improved—by automation. Worse, the workplace becomes an unpleasant and possibly dangerous environment.

The programs that control factory automation, office automation, hospital automation, banking automation—the list is almost endless—must serve three different masters at the same time: the

---

*A. Swasy and C. Hymowitz, "The Workplace Revolution," *The Wall Street Journal*, February 9, 1990, p. R6.

automation system itself; the workers and/or customers who are responsible for controlling the automation system; and the managers who are responsible for the entire process.

In an automated environment, workers make more decisions and have more responsibility, and managers must often give up some of their traditional controls. As a trade-off, however, software provides an information link between managers and workers and furnishes them with a mechanism for tracking and control that is nonintrusive. When every machine on the shop floor is tied to a central information system, managers can obtain a snapshot at any time of production activities. Problem areas can be isolated and corrections made.

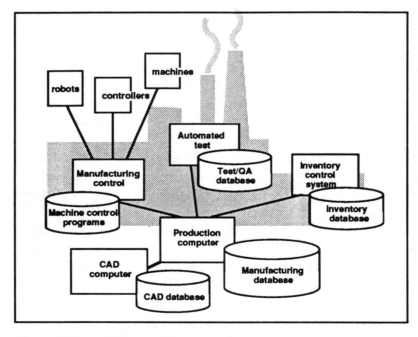

The automated factory is a hierarchy of computer networks that connect machines and information.

The impact of software on manufacturing in the United States has not progressed as rapidly nor has software been adopted as pervasively as many had predicted. In the late 1970s, computer-integrated manufacturing was touted to be the norm by the mid-1980s, and computers, robots, and other automated machines were predicted to bring about a revolution in productivity in the United States. It didn't happen.

The reason for our slow progress has been part economic (management was unwilling to make the monetary commitment to make it happen); part cultural (we were unprepared for the dramatic changes that factory automation demanded in work rules, management, and factory design; and part software (the programs required to link all of the subsystems just weren't there). In fact, the machines were ready, but the systems didn't exist or weren't effective.

So we see that software can be either a catalyst for ongoing change in the workplace or a bottleneck that retards even more significant change. What lies in the future? How will software affect the workplace as the new century approaches?

In the late 1970s, a new phrase was used to describe special keys on a computer's keyboard—they were called *soft keys*. The function of a soft key could change, depending on what the user of the computer terminal was doing and the context of the information being processed. For example, function key number 1 might be used one moment to request a listing of past entries and the next moment to erase an erroneous input. Software manages this change and informs the user of the current meaning of each soft key. Soft keys made interaction more flexible, but could also confuse the user.

As we approach the new century, we'll begin to see *soft jobs* made possible by automation. Workers will no longer spend their day in front of a single-purpose machine. Rather, factories will be filled by an increasing number of programmable machines that can perform many different functions and produce dramatically different components. A textile worker, who used to operate a machine that made one variety of cloth, will control a machine that can produce thirty or forty different varieties. A machinist who once produced a single slotted shaft for a pump mechanism will run a machine that can produce hundreds of different components based on a program that is communicated from a centralized automation system.

Instead of spending every day doing the same thing, the worker's job will become soft—producing different fabrics or different widgets every day. The manner in which the worker interacts with the machine will also become soft, requiring more flexibility, more decision making, and therefore more education. The need for better educated workers will increase the demands on our already overburdened educational system, but as we will see later in this chapter, software may facilitate improvements in our educational processes as well.

In the Office

Most white collar workers interact either directly or indirectly with software-based systems. A business manager reads production reports generated by a database management system, a supervisor uses a project scheduling program to plan work assignments, a financial manager charts assets using a spreadsheet. Currently, the interaction is relatively narrow, and often quite passive. When we communicate with a computer, there is no doubt we are dealing with a machine.

All of that is about to change. Human-computer interfaces have already come a long way, thanks to innovations like the user-friendly menus of the Apple Macintosh,® but there's still more to come. A combination of powerful desktop machines, enormous memory capacity, high resolution display devices, speech recognition, handwriting recognition, and massive amounts of storage capable of holding video, audio, graphic, and text information will provide the foundation for interfaces that may well revolutionize the white collar workplace.

To illustrate how these interfaces might work, we'll provide a look inside the office of the twenty-first century.

"Good morning," you say as you enter the office.

Your workstation screen brightens, a window opens on the screen, an androgynous face appears, and a very human voice says, "Good morning. You have six voice mail messages, two facsimile transmissions, a videogram, and a list of daily action items."

The face and the voice belong to your *information agent,* an interface program that performs a variety of sophisticated clerical duties. It has been customized to anticipate your needs, recognize your voice, and can do many things at once—acting as your interface to the outside world, looking up information, communicating directly with you, and performing other infomation processing functions.

"Show me the action items and today's appointment calendar," you say.

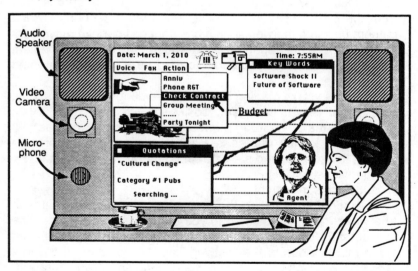

A twenty-first century personalized workstation.

Immediately the list of action items appears on the display and the agent begins to read the list aloud, highlighting each item as it is read. The calendar appears in another window on the display.

"Silence please, and hold the list," you interrupt. "Check voice mail or fax transmissions for key words."

You have just asked the agent to analyze each incoming message to look for any of a set of key words (these could be people's names, places, phone numbers, or topics that you deem important). Scanning the list of action items on the screen, you see two appointments, a few telephone calls to be made, and an anniversary present to be purchased.

After you scan the list, the agent reappears on the screen.

It's early and you're not yet tuned into the work day. Embarrassed (but why should you be, you're communicating with a machine!), you ask, "What did I ask you to do?"

"You asked me to check any of the voice mail or fax transmissions for key words. Would you like a list?"

"Yes, but only those with reference to *Software Shock II.*" A list of messages appears on your screen. You fix on one item from the list and say, "Open." In less than a second, a video camera built into the workstation has tracked your eye movement at the time you said open, and the system has detected the item you were looking at. You begin to read for a few moments and then stop.

The note you're reading refers to the videogram. "Two things, please, " you say to the agent. "I'd like the videogram now. Also, please find me at least ten quotes on the topic *cultural change.* Time frame for the quotes is 1900 to the present. Store the quotes, the source, and the date and generate an action item for me to review them."

"OK," says the agent.

A window appears on the screen and a video presentation (the videogram), transmitted to you by a colleague, begins. The presentation contains sophisticated animation, graphics, and video that is close to the "network quality" common in the late 1980s. Yet it was created on a workstation similar to yours with software that makes the job easy.

While you're viewing the videogram, the agent will have an "apprentice" look for your quotations (in computing jargon: the agent "spawns" a task to perform the library functions you requested). Sources such as *Bartlett's Quotations, The Encyclopedia of American Humor, The Book of Science and Natural Quotes* are readily available. Within seconds, the agent returns to do your bidding. Simultaneously, the first apprentice is searching the database.

"Let me have a word processor," you say to the agent. A word processing program, not unlike the best you see today, appears on the screen. You begin dictating a letter (the keyboard or a handwriting tablet can also be used). The text appears on the screen as you speak each word. While you are dictating, you think of something for the agent to do. Using a pointing device, you click on the agent's window.

"I need a table of all of last year's software sales in the U.S. by quarter. Insert it at the marker I'll note in the document I'm working on. Also, call my publisher and tell them I'll be transmitting the document later today."

"Okay," responds the agent. Apprentices are spawned to generate the table and make the call while you return to your dictation.

The dialogue may be different, the information agent may be somewhat less capable, but the interface we've just described will be a reality.

The interface will be *your* interface, customized to your needs. It will know your work habits, understand the rhythm of your commands, and take care of lots of things while you work on something else. You'll treat it like a human being, possibly give it a name, talk to it as if it were a person. And behind the scenes, software makes it all happen.

Monogrammed and Other Customized Products

Many of us like to see our mark on the things we acquire. Whether it's a dress shirt, personalized stationery, a vanity plate for an automobile, or a beer mug, monogrammed products are often perceived to have more value than those that have not been customized for the purchaser. Monogrammed products cost more and take longer to acquire, but the personal touch compels many to make the purchase.

Today, though monogrammed products are fairly common, truly customized products are relatively rare. Customization demands special attention at every level, from the customer who must specify what is required to the product builder who must adapt a vanilla design to meet the requirements. That's why customized products are expensive.

However, software is about to change all this. We predict the twenty-first century will be an era of customization. Flexible factories, flexible systems, and flexible services will enable consumers in every sector to acquire products that have been specifically customized to their needs.

Using computer-integrated manufacturing (CIM) techniques, the makers of industrial equipment are already moving in this direction. Programmable machine tools, industrial robots, flexible assembly lines, and a variety of other computer-based systems enable each product built to meet the exact requirements of a specific customer. Giants in the aerospace, computer, petrochemical, automotive, machine tool, food processing, and steel industries all use CIM techniques to customize their manufacturing processes. Control systems coordinate the interplay of machines, material, and personnel. The *lights out factory*—a factory that requires no people, just computers, software, and machines—is coming closer to reality.* *Just-in-time* material acquisition strategies keep inventories low and costs down. As a result, product life cycles are compressed and production volume reduced. The process and the product have become customized.

---

*This is a dream for some and a nightmare for many. The displacement of blue collar workers by software can be a major negative side effect. This problem is discussed more in Chapter 3.

But flexible manufacturing techniques and customization are not the sole province of industry giants. Brothers Sports Shop, a small family-owned business in Louisville, Kentucky, wouldn't appear to be a hot bed for flexible manufacturing, but it is.

> As you pass through a store filled with baseball gloves and tennis rackets, hockey skates and football equipment, you'd never guess that buried in the basement of the store, behind thousands of blank athletic jerseys, jackets, and T-shirts, is a flexible manufacturing operation that has made Brothers a regional leader in the sports apparel embroidery business.
>
> Sports teams throughout the region contact Brothers when team and player names must be embroidered on their uniforms. Companies and schools also order logos that are created and stitched into fabric. In the old days, embroidery was painstakingly slow and very expensive. Today, this small sports shop makes use of programmable embroidery equipment to turn out customized products in both large and small quantities, quickly and relatively inexpensively.

The machines that Brothers uses today are not easy to program, and for this reason, customization is economical only if a customer wants to buy more than one piece of apparel. But even this is beginning to change. Soon, a customer will be able to walk into a store like Brothers and use a color high-resolution interactive computer graphics system to draw a design for custom embroidery on a piece of clothing. The system will automatically clean up the design, making it look professional. It also might suggest changes in placement or scaling, get final approval, and then transmit the design to an automated embroidery machine that would create unique apparel for immediate purchase.

Similar interactive systems are already being used to help consumers select furniture, wallpaper, kitchen cabinets, clothing, plastic surgery, vacation itineraries, investment strategies, and a variety of other products and services. In every case, it is computer software that creates the images, makes the suggestions, and diagnoses the problems that will enable consumers to customize a product or service to meet their specific needs.

Customized Information

As the 1990s progress, a new and potentially more important area of product and service customization will see explosive growth. Every modern society will begin to consume customized information on a massive scale.

> The year is 1998. Bill Trippitt has always wanted to grow hybrid orchids, and now that his retirement is approaching, he'd like to get started. Ten years ago, he would have visited a bookstore or a library to gather information on orchids. Now his approach is radically different. Trippitt walks into the family room and switches on the television set. Because his cable company has converted to fiber optics, he can interact with the cable's *Information Store.* The *Information Store* gives new meaning to the phrase "pay TV."
>
> The cable box next to the TV is actually a sophisticated personal computer. Through a series of interactions that combine voice and hand-written input, Trippitt asks for general information about hybrid orchids, as well as specifics on where to purchase them, and how to grow and breed them.
>
> In response, the cable box provides both visual and audio prompts to help him refine his requirements and to suggest different types of presentation formats. Bill chooses a video presentation format for the overview, and written form for the other information so that he can study it at his leisure. The cable box transmits Bill's requirements to the *Information Store's* central computers, and a customized information package is prepared.
>
> Searching its vast library of video presentations, the *Information Store* finds three different video programs produced on orchid growing and orchids in general. It also finds 18,000 pages of information on orchids and extracts and summarizes salient

points into a 180-page "laser book" that will be produced on Bill's color laser fax machine. A complex billing algorithm computes the cost of the information that Bill wants. The entire packet costs $52—slightly more than the cost of a hardcover book. He decides to watch one of the video presentations on orchids now and requests the laser book be printed overnight (when data transmission costs are lower).

By 1999, the customized information industry will be growing at forty to fifty percent per year. By 2005, consumers in the industrial and public marketplace will be able to acquire customized print or electronic magazines, customized entertainment (in which the plot may be controlled by choices made by the viewer), customized music programming, and a variety of other customized information products. In fact, the distinction between information and entertainment will fade as customers gain increasing control over what they see and when they see it.

Navigating a Sea of Information: Storm Warnings

Tony Imperatore is a senior market analyst for a global credit information bureau. He can do a complete credit and demographic profile on any person whose name is submitted by the bureau's client. He's been with the company since 1996 and has been promoted because he is a good "navigator."

"I picked up the structure of the databases very quickly," says Imperatore. "In the early 1990s, all of the data were there, but they weren't connected. Even when you found a database that contained part of what you needed, you had to formulate your queries in a specific way or you'd get nothing worthwhile. Today, it's all fairly automatic, but a good knowledge of the databases still helps."

The databases that Imperatore is talking about contain records on more than 750 million people worldwide. Given a person's name and other identification, he now can navigate geographically diverse databases and collect information on purchases, communications, banking transactions, legal episodes, medical information, travel, and entertainment. Once collected, this information can be analyzed, cross-referenced, and associated with other linked information.

For example, based on a telephone inquiry, an automobile company requests market information on John Doe. Tony Imperatore runs a standard credit report, buying-habit profile, and income statement. Credit information qualifies Doe as a good prospect, but the client also wants a more detailed "associative analysis." So Imperatore searches some more.

Telephone records indicate that Doe also called for information on two competitive car models (now the client can infer the models it's up against) and made several telephone calls to Jane Smith, who, it turns out, bought one of the client's cars. Is Doe asking Smith for advice? The information from the associative analysis is transmitted to software at the automobile company, which generates a personalized letter sent to Doe. It begins:

Dear Mr. Doe:

We are pleased that you are considering the Acme Auto Starlite model for your next new car. We are happy to inform you that your excellent credit entitles you to the following purchase incentives. ...

As you probably know, your friend Jane Smith purchased a Starlite five months ago. Our records indicate that except for routine maintenance, Jane Smith has encountered no problems with her Starlite. In fact, her response to our customer satisfaction questionnaire gives us very high marks.

We'd like to compare the Starlite to the Utopia and the Ventana models in an effort to help you make your purchase decision. ...

Software is the kernel of the information collection, analysis, and dispersal system described above. However, its ability to create customized information also has a down side, leading to an unparalleled potential for invasion of privacy. Are such activities intrusive? Many civil libertarians argue they are, but many business people salivate at the thought of such targeted marketing data. Are techniques such as these already in use in a somewhat less elaborate form? Absolutely.

In Search of New Modes of Education

> Professor Steven Millhouse paces back and forth in front of a classroom of university students who eagerly listen to a lecture on European political history. As Millhouse lectures, the students scribble notes on important points. Occasionally, a student will ask a question. Millhouse comes from the old school, and his responses tend to be formal and abbreviated. He prefers delivering the planned lecture and does an acceptable job of presenting the material. At the end of class, Millhouse announces a midterm examination for the following week. Students gather their belongings and prepare to trudge across campus to their next class. The year is 1697. The place is Oxford University in England.

This description of Millhouse and his class would change only slightly if, three hundred years later, we visited any one of hundreds of colleges and universities in the United States. Sure, we use slightly more sophisticated materials, and the number of available courses has expanded dramatically, but the dynamics of the classroom have changed little. Students still take notes (often instead of listening). Teachers, lecturing alone, present information at an even pace—they cannot slow down for some students while at the same time speeding up for others. They must try to give individual students as much attention as possible within the context of limited time and limited resources. If the teacher is outstanding, the educational experience is also outstanding, but if the teacher is mediocre or worse, the educational experience suffers proportionally. In fact, many of us can think of more than one course in which the teacher contributed almost nothing to our learning. On the other hand, we all remember the truly excellent teachers we have encountered throughout our lives.

Many lay people and educators look at our current mode of education and argue there is no better approach. While they'll admit that many elements of the system need to be improved, the human relationship between teachers and students, to them, is the best possible method. We agree that the teacher–student relationship is integral to good learning, but we also believe the definition of "teacher" will change dramatically over the next century to include both people and software power.

Lewis Perelman, director of the Hudson Institute's Project Learning 2001, reports, "Two decades of research show that computer-based instruction produces at least thirty percent more learning in forty percent less time at thirty percent less cost than traditional classroom teaching." He goes on: "U.S. schools and colleges are technologically stuck in the Middle Ages for much the same reason the Soviet collective farms are: a complete lack of accountability to the consumer and total insulation from competitive market forces."* Harsh words, but arguably on target.

Today's use of computers in education barely scratches the surface of their potential. At the primary and secondary levels, computers are often used as sophisticated "flip card" machines, helping students to drill in rather tedious fashion. The way in which software is currently used at all educational levels will have little to do with the way that it will be used after the year 2000. However, because change is so often slow, software's impact on education will not be revolutionary, but evolutionary.

The key to effective use of computers in education is *courseware*. Courseware encompasses all information to be presented on a specific topic—the appropriate facts that students must learn, supplementary information that motivates their learning, drills that reinforce learning, and an interactive mechanism that enables students to find answers to common questions, skip information and/or facts

---

*L.J. Perelman, "Luddite Schools Wage a Wasteful War," *The Wall Street Journal*, Sept. 10, 1990, p. A14.

that are known, and select a learning mode that is best suited to the individual student's learning abilities.

Educational theorists believe that different people learn using different modalities. Some learn best by reading; others learn best when information is presented in an audio format. Some require dynamic visual stimulation, while others need static facts presented in a repetitive fashion. Experts tell us there may be hundreds of combinations of learning styles.* The best courseware would accommodate not one but all of these modes of learning. It would enable the student to customize both the learning mode and the information contained within a lesson. This courseware is software-based and would include the following kinds of systems.

Authoring systems will enable educators to create mixed media presentations that bring educational information to students. *Presentation systems* will deliver the courseware to students individually. *Monitoring systems* will summarize the information covered, the types of interaction the student made, and the results of any drills, quizzes, or tests managed by the software.

The problem, of course, has nothing to do with hardware technology and everything to do with software technology. In fact, software offers the promise for the development of advanced educational approaches and at the same time remains a bottleneck for the development of such approaches. It takes enormous effort to develop effective software to perform these functions and (using today's information retrieval technology) even greater effort to develop meaningful courseware once the underlying software base has been established.

Software developers lack the necessary insight and experience with education, and educators lack understanding of the possibilities software has to offer. The bottleneck can be broken by forming cooperative teams of educators and software developers and freeing

---

*E.J. Coe, *Creating an Holistic Developmentally Responsive Learning Environment,* University Microfiche Inc., 1988.

time for them to do some creative thinking. Part of the problem is there is no central information store. If a teacher wants to build a course on the geography of Asia, for example, it would be nice to have available all *National Geographic* videos produced on countries in that region. The teacher also needs access to maps, population statistics, political information, and so forth. Today there is no easy access to such information. The teacher (courseware designer) must gather the information, organize it into a form suitable for automated presentation, and then test the results on students. Our overburdened and underpaid teachers are not motivated to do this work.

Industry looks at the problem differently. If a major company spends $1 million annually on employee training, a five percent improvement in training productivity translates into a savings of $50 thousand. We believe the impetus for educational change may not be the schools, but rather high-technology industry. Companies throughout the United States spend billions annually on formal and informal training. They recognize that to deal with the fundamental changes occuring in the workplace over the next few decades, the work force will have to become more knowledgeable, more educated, more sophisticated, and more flexible. When total education budgets are considered, companies throughout the U.S. spend more than three hundred times as much on computer-based education as our public schools do.

Yet, even with these massive expenditures, major companies train in much the same way as they did ten, twenty, or even fifty years ago. But as the financial burden of training increases, many companies will begin to look for new approaches. Unlike public and private educational institutions, which are notoriously short on funds, technology companies can allocate the financial resources to improve education delivery systems while decreasing costs in the long term. Already a number of small companies are hard at work on next-generation computer-based instruction systems touted to reduce training costs while at the same time improve learning. The computer-based education systems developed in the private sector over the next few decades may serve as a basis for educational changes in the public sector throughout the first century of the new millennium.

The Little Red School House

April 7, 2022, 7:55 A.M., Houston, Texas. Susan Smith (age 13) waves a cheerful "Bye, mom!" as she steps from the transporter onto the pavement of the dropoff area for the South Branch LC ("learning center" or what we would call a school). She turns and watches while her friend Mary Chu (age 12) gathers her belongings and stuffs them into a nylon shoulder sack bearing a picture of their favorite pop singing group. The two girls step onto a small wooden bridge that disappears into a well-manicured wooded area. They cross the bridge, pass through the woods, and walk across a small meadow to the door of a modern building that blends well with its natural surroundings.

They enter South Branch LC and are greeted by their educational director, Ms. Meltzer. Other students have already arrived and can be seen working in a variety of areas, but the most unusual feature of the classroom is a number of cubicle structures that vaguely resemble library carrels from the twentieth century. Several students are engrossed in activity within these structures, while others chat quietly in group activities.

The two girls put away their belongings and join several students seated in a circle. Within a few minutes the other students join the circle. Ms. Meltzer talks a bit about the day's activities, but for the most part the students lead the discussion. After twenty minutes, the group breaks up and each person moves off to an individual activity. Susan Smith walks to one of the carrels and says "Hello, this is Susan."

The walls and desk top of the carrel glow with a warm light and a pleasant voice responds, "Good morning, Susan, what would you like to work on today?" At the same time, the desk top shows a histogram of the various learning tasks she has planned for this month and the percentage completed of each. Susan's educational plan is set through consultation with Ms. Meltzer and is based on a combination of objectives required by the state education system and areas of particular interest to Susan. Once Susan has chosen her work plan for the month, Ms. Meltzer draws on a variety of educational software tools that she combines with her own experience and knowledge of Susan's learning style to create a customized curriculum for the student.

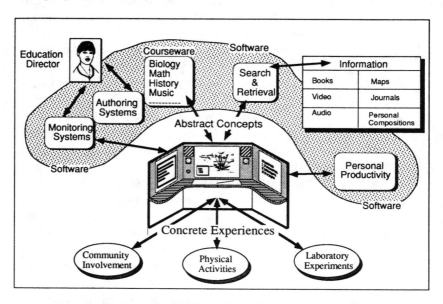

In a twenty-first century Learning Center, a learning carrel serves as the junction of both concrete and abstract experiences.

Susan scans the histogram in the desk top and makes a mental note to tackle the Texas History project in the afternoon but for now she chooses, "Biology, please!" Quickly the histogram disappears and up pops the color image of a plant in cross section, the point in the biology curriculum that Susan was last studying.

The soft voice of the carrel begins, "The primary factors controlling plant growth ..." Because Susan is an auditory learner, she has the learning carrel speak to her, but Mary in a nearby carrel prefers to read the text of most information. Susan cocks her head to one side as she hears the word "nutrients" and touches a glowing spot on the desk top. The images and voice of the biology curriculum pause and a display appears explaining nutrients. Susan studies the nutrients display and remembers the earlier experiments that she and Mary performed with living plants outside in the garden. Another touch of the desk top retrieves the graphs prepared last month as part of the write-up of the experiment. On the back wall of the carrel, the video recording she made of Mary planting the seeds appears. After several minutes, she nods to herself, brushes her fingers over the desk top, and the biology curriculum resumes.

As Susan continues her biology study, a student in a nearby carrel searches through the collections of the Library of Congress contained on a single silver disk for references on the importance of an informed populace to an effective democratic government. A music buff in another carrel is creating his own recording of Mozart, Bach, Buddy Holly, and some modern compositions to use as background music for his video paper on twentieth century art. Another student with a strong right arm and quick reflexes retrieves the batting averages of major league baseball players and correlates them to determine the team with the highest probability of winning the division title. This prediction will complete his math work for the month.

Several miles away on the local college campus, the older brothers and sisters of these children can be found using similar technology to model geologic sedimentation, experimentally fly spacecraft designs, or study the literary merits of several modern authors. Meanwhile the teachers, freed from many record keeping and testing tasks by the learning carrels, can devote their attention to monitoring the progress of each student and interacting with individuals and groups on a personal basis.

Will the little red school house evolve to become the image that we have painted? Only if there is a concerted national effort akin to the space program to make it happen. Central to this effort will be the development of a new generation of software that promotes, monitors, coordinates, and controls learning. Should the little red school house evolve in the way that we've described? That's a topic for another book!

Communications

In the 1960s movie classic *The Graduate,* Dustin Hoffman plays a young man who is about to learn the ways of the world. In an unforgettable scene in which he is being counseled on his future in business, a boorish businessman advises him with a single word, "Plastics." If that scene were played today, the word might be "Communications."

Worldwide, we are experiencing a communications revolution, and again software resides as its technical kernel. Communications technology allows us to watch Boris Becker at the moment he serves for the match at the Australian Open; to conduct business from a cellular phone in our car; to receive dozens of fax messages from around the world; to telephone any person in any industrialized nation; to transmit words, voice, pictures, video images, sound, and every other mode of human communication over networks that have become the new highways for commerce.

Yet, communications technology is really nothing new. The first telephone networks were the technological marvel of the 1930s. Computers and software have rejuvenated this "old" technology. Today, a telephone network switch is actually millions of lines of programming language source code and associated computers. The switch communicates with network nodes, each containing still more software. Some are embedded in geosynchronous communications satellites located thousands of miles above our heads.

The futurists of the 1970s talked about a global village in which communication among individuals, businesses, and nations would lead to shared values, shared economies, and ultimately a cohesive, global culture. With the widespread use of communication networks enabled by software, this is already beginning to happen. Just as railroads and later the interstate highway system provided the pathways for commerce during the industrial era, communications networks will provide global pathways for commerce during the information era.

By the mid-1990s, it is estimated that more than 25 million miles of fiber optic cable will have been laid. To understand what this means, consider that a copper wire can carry approximately 48 separate telephone conversations, while an equivalent fiber optic cable can carry 8,000. Fiber optics will allow the bandwidth (that is, volume) of communication to rise dramatically. Stated simply, this means the worldwide communications network will be able to accommodate much more traffic—and it had better, because the communications demand of the twenty-first century will likely be orders of magnitude greater than today

To accommodate the profound changes in the workplace, the evolution of monogrammed products, the rapid growth of an information delivery industry, and even the changes in our educational system, high bandwidth communications—implemented on a global system of computer networks—will be required.

Networks have a way of amplifying collective knowledge, but they also have a way of amplifying problems. As our reliance on networks grows, we need to consider the dark side, as evidenced by the following recent real-life situations.

A Network Collapse: The Case of the Wandering Bug

In December 1989, AT&T installed new software in 114 long-distance telephone switches intended to improve error recovery efficiency (a network switch is a computer-based control center that routes long-distance telephone traffic). Unfortunately, the new software had a latent defect (a bug) that was undiscovered despite extensive testing.

On the morning of January 15, 1990, one of the network switches experienced an unusual hardware fault. Following the protocol contained in the new software, the switch that experienced the fault signaled another switch to take over its load and attempted to reset itself. But the latent bug in the software transmitted another unintelligible message that the second switch perceived as an error. It sent the same erroneous message to a third switch and attempted to reset itself. Within minutes, the defect had propagated throughout the AT&T long-distance telephone network. All 114 switches were paralyzed. Business communication—telephone calls, fax, computer-to-computer communication, video traffic—ground to a halt. Although analysts argue about the cost, most believe that AT&T lost between $20 and $50 million in revenue during the ten hours it took to correct the problem. The total amount of lost business and confusion for its customers has never been accurately estimated.

There's an interesting postscript to this story as related by Peter Neumann: During congressional testimony on the technological safety of the software for the Strategic Defense Initiative (SDI) system (and prior to the AT&T network failure), an AT&T scientist "asserted that a large, robust, and resilient SDI system could be designed and implemented, because it could use the demonstrably sound techniques found in the U.S. public telecommunications network."*

As networks of interconnected computers become the predominant architecture for large computer-based systems, the danger of error propagation grows. A small error in the software of one computer can propagate throughout the network causing hundreds or possibly thousands of machines to stop functioning. The results can

---

*P.G. Neumann, "Inside Risks: Some Reflections on a Telephone Switching Problem," *Communications of the ACM,* Vol. 33, No. 7 (July 1990), p. 154.

range from inconvenience to disaster. Imagine what could happen if the problem were caused purposely!

A Network Collapse: Malicious Mischief

On November 2, 1988, Robert Morris, a graduate student at Cornell University, created a self-replicating, self-propagating program called a virus or worm, that was injected into Internet, a large network of university and government computers. Within hours, the virus had infected more than six thousand computer systems throughout the United States. The computers and the network ground to a halt. Thousands of hours of working time were lost by those who had to deal with the virus. Morris was indicted and convicted of violations of Federal law.

The scourge of computer viruses is amplified because the damage isn't limited to a single machine but can affect all machines (nodes) of the network—including all the people who must work on them. Many experts believe that our networks are vulnerable to malevolent attack, what some have called "technoterrorism." In fact, "cyber–punk" books with titles such as *Shockwave Rider, Neuromancer,* and *Wetware* encourage would-be computer hackers with fictional heroes that ride the networks of the world leaving dismay and destruction at every turn. Software is a potent weapon of the hacker and the terrorist. But software will also be part of our defense.

A Global Economy

The cover story of a news magazine blares, "They're Buying America!" An editorial in a major newspaper laments the trade deficit. Business people talk of the European Economic Community as the United States of Europe. Great Britain, Germany, Japan, Korea—each our economic partner and our economic competitor.

Yet all of this may disappear during the first decades of the twenty-first century. We may be moving toward a world economic order—a united countries of the world—and software will have a major role to play.

Capital and foreign exchange controls are already being removed throughout Europe. A banking system, driven by sophisticated transaction processing networks that connect member banks in every country, may ultimately lead to a single European economy or even a single European currency. Without software to manage this process, it would be impossible to accomplish.

The real question is, Will we extrapolate the European model into a world model? Will a global economy in the twenty-first century lead to a world currency? To erasure of international borders? To world political leadership? No one really knows. Business and industry is already moving in that direction. Government (probably dragged kicking and screaming) is likely to follow.

As information becomes an even more important commodity and global communications networks become even more powerful and pervasive, it will become increasingly difficult to control trade and increasingly futile to talk in terms of trade deficits. Here in the United States, we do not talk about trade deficits between New York and California, nor do we become concerned if an Ohio firm buys a Texas factory. Our economy is integrated. In their recent book, *Megatrends 2000,* John Naisbitt and Patricia Aburdene state, "The economic forces of the world are surging across national borders, resulting in more democracy, more freedom, more trade, more opportunity, and greater prosperity."*

Behind much of this surge is the lowly computer program—managing transactions, enabling communication, storing and retriev-

---

*J. Naisbitt and P. Aburdene, *Megatrends 2000* (New York: William Morrow & Co., 1990).

ing data, controlling factories, monitoring trade, supervising travel, guiding strategy, protecting critical systems, directing the flow of commerce. Without software the global economy stops . . . dead.

The Compass

3
Orthogonal Connections

When we look to the future, it is the orthogonal connections that intrigue us most. An orthogonal connection is a discontinuity in the expected progression of things leading to an outcome that was never foreseen. Earlier we talked about automobiles and the mating habits of American teenagers—the connection exists, but it was not at all obvious when the car was invented. An orthogonal connection is not sequential, it is not obvious, it is not easily predicted. To get from here to there, we'll need to take many right angle turns—some that may appear irrational when we look at them today, but will seem very natural when we look backward in the years to come.

At the risk of appearing whimsical, let's try a few orthogonal connections for software to see how it may change the fabric of our lives in the years to come.

Cities and Software

Software is a pivotal technology in communications, as we've seen, and a catalyst for the information era. The orthogonal connection: *Software may lead to the demise of the city center as we currently know it.*

Over the past five hundred or so years, cities have been concentrators, collection points, for people. People have moved to the city to be near factories and commerce and to enjoy the cultural benefits that are centered there. However, the communications revolution and the information era are making concentrations of people much less important: Witness the rise of electronic commuting, the increasing popularity of video conferencing (especially as the cost of travel and fears over terrorism increase), and the rapid growth of direct mail companies.

At the same time, the quality of life in cities has declined as crime, poverty, and the other social ills often associated with heavy concentrations of people have taken their toll. City dwellers have asked themselves, "What am I doing here?" and responded by migrating to the suburbs. Now, because electronic commuting enables them to "travel" at the speed of light, they can move to a small town in Vermont and effectively "work" in New York City. Over time, we predict, increasing numbers of workers who have the education and jobs that allow them this kind of flexibility will move beyond the city limits and often beyond the suburbs. The structure of the city will change dramatically.

Drive By Wire

Software has become a major component in the automobile. It controls the fuel system, braking, engine operations, and dashboard displays of most cars. The orthogonal connection: *Few people will have to know how to drive a car in 2050.*

Traffic delays pump hundreds of thousands of tons of pollutants into the air every month. They cause tens of millions of dollars in lost productivity during the same time span. And they're getting worse in every major metropolitan area.

By the first decade of the twenty-first century, vehicles equipped with computer-based navigation and collision avoidance systems will be relatively commonplace. These will probably lead to a "platooning" capability that will enable vehicles to link together electronically (like the cars of a train), traveling along highways in tandem at very high speeds. Later, more sophisticated software-based systems that refit highways with "pathfinding" capabilities will automatically guide vehicles to their destination. Already, the major automotive companies and electronics giants such as Motorola, IBM, AT&T, Philips, and certain Japanese companies are all quietly exploring intelligent vehicle systems and advanced highway infrastructure design.

As hands-off driving becomes a reality, there will be little reason to know how to drive a car. We'll leave the driving to software.

Artificial Reality

Software is the basis of a major form of escape and entertainment: the video game. Today, the primary consumers of these games haven't yet reached puberty. Tomorrow, as these video game fanatics age, this form of entertainment will likewise mature and evolve to provide new levels of experience. The orthogonal connection: *Software may replace drugs as a safe and socially acceptable hallucinogen.*

The year is 2018 and Itasha Wells decides to take a trip. She'll begin her trip in a small suburb of Atlanta, Georgia, at 7:30:00

P.M. on May 9, and will arrive in the rain forest of Brazil at 7:30:15 P.M. on May 9. She'll spend a few hours exploring the forest and be back by bedtime. Her entire trip will be "virtual." Wells is about to experience *artificial* or *virtual reality.*

She will use the latest consumer toy for her trip—an *artificial reality unit* or ARU. The ARU is no larger than a VCR, and accepts CD-like cartridges available for rent or purchase in electronic entertainment shops. Connected to the ARU is a helmet-like apparatus that displays images on miniature wraparound high-definition TVs and produces advanced stereo sound through speakers at the ears. The helmet is tethered electronically to the ARU and has electromechanical sensors that detect head motion. "Electrogloves" are worn on the hands and feet. As she stands on a multi-directional treadmill, she activates the ARU, first customizing her trip from a menu that she sees in front of her. Her trip begins.

Every turn of her head and every step that she takes lets her experience the sights, the sounds, and even the smells of the tropical rain forest. Her guide points out rare species of plants and animals, and she reaches her hand out to touch them. Itasha Wells *is* in the rain forest.

Artificial reality will become the video game of the second decade of the next century. Anyone will be able to buy a trip to almost anywhere inexpensively and can see every important building, museum, city, and landmark on earth—and it will take only an evening to do it! Other consumers will be able to buy adventure trips, when they will face some peril and live to tell about it. This combination of video and computer graphics will be generated by software. Every response to human motion will be managed by software. Every sound, every reaction, everything will be produced and controlled by software.

By 2020, companies will begin to create "unreal" trips—trips that will conjure up long lost memories of LSD, mescaline, and designer drugs. Objects will distort and change color in frighteningly powerful imagery. Time will slow and race forward. Sounds will rise and fall in surreal fashion. New worlds will be created, and many people won't be able to get enough. They will spend hours, sometimes days, inside their ARU. Some people will become concerned. These unreal trips will do no damage to the body—but to the tripper, the AR *will seem* real, and be possibly addictive.

The advance of this technology may cause us to change our fundamental notion of reality. After all, whether you sense a distant planet's surface with human eyes at a distance of six feet, with robot sensors at a distance of a hundred million miles, or via a realistic computer graphics simulation from a few inches away, is the experience more or less real? Software can distort or enhance what is real, and that raises some interesting philosophical questions about reality, fidelity, and truth. Perhaps the meaning of reality will shift over time to convey more about the degree of control over possible outcomes rather than notions about physical presence or absence of human sensory inputs.

Software Psychosis

Software gives the current generation of intelligent products a crude personality. Just as it is difficult to interact with a person who has a disagreeable personality, it is stressful to interact with VCRs, personal computers, ATMs, and hundreds of other products whose software personality is disagreeable. The orthogonal connection: *Software-based machines may evolve personalities so agreeable that humans will form significant relationships with them.*

In the science fiction cult film *Blade Runner,* Harrison Ford plays a bounty hunter who must eliminate a group of renegade androids (automatons in human form). Toward the end of this intriguing tale, Ford develops a believable love relationship with a software-based machine that both looks and acts very human.

In the future, as people interact with such intelligent machines, some undoubtedly will form bizarre human-machine friendships, in some cases to the exclusion of other human relationships. Such behavior may even spawn a specialized field of abnormal psychology.

Software and Human Evolution

Software has played a role in every major advance in genetics since the double helix was discovered. Within the next several decades, supercomputers, running programs containing sophisticated genetic decoding algorithms, will map the complete DNA code. The orthogonal connection: *Software could lead to a race of human beings that dominate every field of endeavor.*

Using limited maps of the DNA code, geneticists will soon be able to modify genes that carry inherited maladies such as sickle cell anemia, cystic fibrosis, and diabetes. As software becomes more sophisticated during the next century and as knowledge accumulates in this area, detailed maps of every human gene will provide more and more ways that man can control what nature has chosen.

Will the specter of a genetically engineered human come to pass? Will we be able to select designer eye color, optimal height and musculature, hair texture, intelligence? Will we want to do this? The debate about the overwhelming implications of such genetic engineering will not be resolved soon—and rightfully so, because we are discussing intervention in the very evolution of our species.

The Way We Think

Not long ago, a business acquaintance who was unfamiliar with computers asked me (SRH) for advice concerning a home computer. Having already done his homework, he merely wanted confirmation that the system he chose for his home was a good one and that it would meet his requirements. The configuration he described was a fine one indeed, including the latest, most powerful processor, color monitor, plenty of memory, ample hard disk, and a laser printer. (I secretly envied him his impressive system.) I told him with confidence that the system would satisfy his requirements for a home computer.

Several months later, I saw him at a conference and asked how he was getting along with his new computer. Like a proud father, he told me all the great things he was doing with the machine and its numerous software packages. I listened patiently and came away with a new perspective from his closing comment.

"You know," he said, "I never thought of doing the things I'm now doing with the computer until I had one available. It really has changed the way I think."

Software has changed the way he acquires and interprets information. In our many years of observing new computer users, we have seen many people change their thinking process (usually for the better) through the use of computer software. Whether the user is a scientist or a stockbroker, a student or a secretary, an educator or a business manager—all have tapped the power that software brings to their mental processes.

Complex mathematical models (implemented in software) perform calculations beyond human capabilities and redirect our thinking. For example, spacecraft navigation requires complex computation at speeds beyond the capacity of the human mind. Now that software has given us the ability to navigate in space, we can evaluate close up video images of the outer planets, probe the origins of the universe, and consider travel beyond our planet.

At the other end of the spectrum, the lowly spreadsheet allows business people to consider countless options that would have been impossible before. A word processor with a spelling and grammar checker allows college students to devote more time and thought to research and less to the laborious task of manually writing down ideas on paper. A modeling program in a high school chemistry laboratory sparks the imagination of teenagers and changes their attitudes toward science. A home accounting package gives ordinary home owners a level of financial control and planning previously available only from professional accountants. A graphics package allows architects to communicate with their clients with a clarity never before possible.

In all of these examples, software changes the way people think. Because new software applications are limited only by the imagination and creativity of its designers, the twenty-first century will be the beginning of many new pathways for the mind.

The Quest for HAL

In 1968, filmmaker Stanley Kubrick and futurist Arthur C. Clarke teamed to create *2001: A Space Odyssey*. In this science fiction classic, we meet HAL (for Heuristically programmed ALgorithmic computer), an anthropomorphic computer that has come to represent all that is good and bad about the future of computers and software. In our society, HAL is repeatedly referenced with reverence, disgust, and sometimes fear. In Clarke's novel,[*] HAL represents all that software might become—the good, the bad, and the ugly.

In the years since the film's human hero, Dr. David Bowman, shut down HAL's higher functions, we have not progressed as rapidly as Clarke envisioned in either computer or space technology. Moreover, it is highly unlikely that functionality as sophisticated as HAL will be achieved by the start of the new century.

Elements of HAL, driven by advances in both hardware and software technologies, are beginning to surface. Computer voice communication is approaching practical application. Graphic user interfaces make communication with the computer's software more intuitive. Real-time process control has been implemented in many factories and especially in spacecraft. Robotics has become a significant industry itself. Expert systems offer some meager forms of reasoning and help with some medical diagnoses, for example. Neural network technology shows some early indications that computers can indeed learn.

---

[*]A.C. Clarke, *2001: A Space Odyssey* (New York: New American Library, 1968).

Hardware continues its dizzying advance. Recent history indicates that we can expect the power of a fixed-price computer to double every two years. If this two-year doubling phenomenon is to continue for many decades, major shifts in technology, occurring every twenty years or so, will be required.

Using this simple doubling rule, we can confidently expect the desktop computer to be capable of a hundred million instructions per second by 1999. This would be a hundred times more powerful than the most common business computer in use today.

Extrapolating from this rule, Susan Smith of South Branch LC (in 2022) can expect her learning carrel to be 65,000 times more powerful than today's classroom computer. However, if the trend of the past few years continues (computer power doubling in *less* than two years), Susan Smith could be using a computer that is a million times more powerful than those available today!

Intelligent Machines

Even though we will not see HAL by 2001, the next century will certainly see computers that exhibit intelligent behavior (although what constitutes "intelligence" is open to debate). As a consequence, we will need to address the issues originally raised by Isaac Asimov in his collection of short stories *I, ROBOT* and explored in many subsequent novels by him as well as others.[*]

Among Asimov's questions are, Do intelligent machines have rights? How will humans relate to machines that are potentially more intelligent than their creators? If machines can supply all basic human needs (food, clothing, and shelter), what will humans do with their time—create or vegetate?

If you think these questions are best left for some future generation, consider this report some five months before the Gulf War:

---

[*]I. Asimov, *I, ROBOT* (New York: Doubleday & Co., 1950).

(From Channel 4 news, London, 28th Aug 90): It is reported that Iraq may be deploying some of the Royal Navy's latest high-tech weaponry. Apparently this is causing US commanders to be reluctant to send aircraft carriers into the northern area of the Gulf.

The villain of the piece is the smart mine "Stonefish," developed by Marconi Underwater Systems under contract to the Royal Navy. This little charmer is so cute it listens to the engine noise of ships passing overhead, and can tell what type of vessel is within range. It "hides" from minesweepers, and blows the backside off anything else. At the heart of the system is (you've guessed it!) "highly sophisticated and classified" *software.* [*]

Western military forces created a relatively unsophisticated robot, but in the wrong hands, it was turned on its creators. What will happen as robotic weapons become even more sophisticated? We should begin thinking about Asimov's questions now.

Social Consequences

Software is a primary driving force behind the changes in the workplace. There is no doubt that automated factories and offices will change the nature of work as we now know it. There is also little debate that people will be displaced in the process. For years, commentators have argued the benefits and dangers of workplace automation. On the one hand, automation can lead to improved profit and global competitiveness. This in turn leads to a more robust economy in which new jobs and a better economic climate are created for all. On the other hand, automation eliminates many unskilled jobs. The work force must become better educated to survive. What if the work force fails to attain higher levels of education? Fewer jobs, coupled with social and economic upheaval, will be the result.

---

[*]P. Mellor, "Risks to the Public in Computers and Related Systems," P.G. Neumann, moderator. *ACM Sigsoft Notes,* Vol. 15, No. 5 (October 1990), p. 14.

Will we evolve into a two-class society, one of displaced low-skilled workers with nothing to do, and another of highly educated professionals and managers who suffer from the stress of over-whelming responsibility?* Alternatively, will automation free people for innovative and creative pursuits and create a modern Renaissance without poverty or ignorance? Will machines that change the way we think bring us neuroses or new horizons? Will innovations in education systems bring new opportunities to improve literacy and understanding or will the cost of such systems stratify the population into a wealthy supereducated elite and an undereducated poor?

Government and industrial leaders occasionally try to address these issues, but platitudes seem to be all that result. To date, such leadership has failed to develop strategies to address the needs of all segments of our population in the twenty-first century. If we react when the problems become untenable, it will be too late.

The Millennium Cometh

The entire fabric of our lives will be affected by computer software as we approach the twenty-first century. This may be hyperbole, but we feel it is a foregone conclusion. Think about it: Our economy, products, homes, cars, schools, transportation, health care, entertainment, national defense, political systems, modes of communication, books, newspapers, language, art, even the way we think, all will be affected by computer software.

Now, armed with this vision of the future, we need to step back to see how we've gotten to where we are today. Then, once the technology is bracketed in time, we'll be ready to explore the people and processes responsible for creating the new driving force.

---

*Kurt Vonnegut explores this possibility in *Player Piano* (New York: Delacorte Press, 1952).

Part II
Origins

In the last thirty years, companies in all the industrialized nations have reaped the benefits and suffered the inadequacies of computer software. As a technology, software has grown from an ill-defined intangible inside a computer to an engineered systems component that is often more important and more costly than the computer itself.

As a business, software has been transformed from a cottage industry into a multibillion dollar international enterprise. As a management concern, software has evolved from a technical activity better left in the back room into a strategic business issue sometimes debated in the boardroom.

Software has come a long way, but its beginnings were modest. Originally treated as an incidental issue, software soon became recognized as the driving force behind the computer revolution. Today, we look at software and see not one but two images: first, a powerful technology that has shaped our world; and second, a bottleneck that retards the evolution of even more powerful technology.

The Electronic Autumn

4
In the Beginning

What's past is prologue.

—William Shakespeare, *The Tempest*

The past is but the beginning of a beginning, and all that is and has been is but the twilight of the dawn.

—H.G. Wells, *The Discovery of the Future*

When you consider the history of the computer, you get the feeling you're watching a snowball rolling downhill. Beginning in the 1950s, the computer snowball began to roll. At first, its progress was steady, but slow. A new generation of computers appeared every five to seven years, and the technology proliferated throughout business, government, and industry. Things appeared to be under control.

Each new generation of hardware spawned its own family of software applications. But while the hardware was thrown away, programs from earlier generations of hardware were often adapted to run on the newer machines. Software remained as an artifact of an earlier era. This migration of software across computer generations seemed innocent enough. After all, why not reuse a program that had already provided benefit for many years? But the artifact became brittle. The continuing reuse of aging programs would become a major burden on an already overburdened software development community.

As the snowball grew and gathered momentum, hardware prices plummeted. Large mainframe computers and moderately sized minicomputers spread across the corporate landscape, and new computer generations arrived every three to four years.

At first, software stayed in the background, trying to keep pace with increasingly more powerful and less expensive hardware. New systems software was built for each new machine generation, and applications software had to be created for new classes of users. The programming staff at many companies quadrupled in size between 1962 and 1975. The typical production library, containing all the different programs used by a company and once numbering fewer than ten different programs, ballooned to having hundreds by the mid-1970s.

The demand for new programs grew even more rapidly, with need for databases, telecommunications, management information systems, computer graphics, process control, automated manufacturing, computer-aided design, and on and on. Limited resources were spread very thin, and a backlog developed.

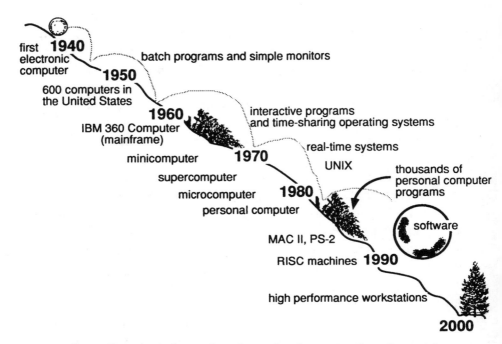

first **1940**
electronic
computer

batch programs and simple monitors

1950

600 computers in
the United States

1960

IBM 360 Computer
(mainframe)

interactive programs
and time-sharing operating systems

minicomputer **1970**

real-time systems

UNIX

supercomputer

thousands of
personal computer
programs

microcomputer **1980**

personal computer

software

MAC II, PS-2

RISC machines **1990**

high performance workstations

2000

Over the past four decades, the impact of software has grown at an ever-accelerating rate, like a snowball rolling downhill out of control.

To meet the demand, companies scrambled to increase the size of their programming departments. But good people were hard to find. Few formal university courses in programming and computer science were offered, and industry training programs were inadequate to fill the demand. As a result, people with backgrounds unrelated to computers were apprenticed to experienced programmers, and on-the-job training helped meet the demand.

The Era of the Mainframe

Each new generation of computers increased the demand for both systems and applications software. When IBM introduced its System 360 mainframe computer in the mid-1960s, for example, the company spent more than a thousand person-years of effort to build the operating system that enabled the machine to function. In addition, its customers had to hire specialists whose sole job was the care and feeding of the operating system.

Hundreds of millions of characters of information were processed by tens of millions of computer instructions at a cost of millions of dollars. Software had clearly become a major line item in the budget.

By the mid-1970s, the snowball was as large as a house and traveling at a frightening speed. Pieces began breaking off and forming other snowballs that began their own journey down the hill. The dominance of the mainframe computer began to fade as vector and parallel computers took over complex computational tasks, and personal computers took over interactive functions (see the Glossary for definitions). Advancing network technology began to handle the data sharing needs of many users.

New Concepts in Small Packages

By 1978, new integrated circuits, called microprocessors, provided ardent groups of computer hobbyists with the raw materials for the construction of home computers. A number of companies grew up virtually overnight to offer a variety of kit computers that could be assembled by anyone with a soldering iron, reasonable intelligence, and no small amount of persistence. Building these computers wasn't hard, but doing anything useful with them was painful at best. There was no personal computer software as we know it today. The best one could do was to develop rudimentary programs using primitive programming languages.

With the exception of the hard-core techies, few people really wanted to build their own computer, yet many had a desire to own one. In response to the desire for ready-to-run machines, several companies began offering "appliance computers," that is, computers that came in a box like a toaster or a microwave oven. Computers, once sold only on a business-to-business basis, were now on sale in the local department store. Although dozens of tiny companies entered this market, only a few have survived and prospered. Only one—Apple Computer—has become a giant, with 1990 worldwide revenue in excess of $5 billion.

The growth in home computers created a demand for applications software. Most people who owned these machines found that programming them wasn't their cup of tea. A cottage industry grew up to supply the demand. As more software became available, computer sales increased. More computer sales pushed the demand for still more software, and the snowball grew in size and accelerated even more. By 1980, the fledgling personal computer market had grown to sufficient size to capture the attention of the biggest of the computer giants, IBM Corporation.

Coming of Age

In 1981, IBM introduced the original IBM PC. The design incorporated the best features of several earlier computers into a single system that brought legitimacy to this young branch of the industry. The confidence inspired by the entry of IBM into the marketplace caused a flood of sales into the business sector, and within two years the IBM PC had established itself as the de facto standard for the industry. More than seven thousand software products have been developed for the IBM PC.

In late 1982, the founders of Compaq Computer realized that the IBM PC could be cloned and began manufacturing PC compatibles at lower prices. The enormous potential of the PC market was demonstrated when Compaq went from nothing to $100 million in revenue in one year! Other clone manufacturers followed, and the resultant price war contributed to the declining cost of the personal computer. Ten years after the introduction of the early appliance computers, a typical personal computer was about twenty times faster and had a memory capacity almost fifteen times greater than the original IBM PC. If this trend continues, personal computers of the next decade could have a billion bytes of memory, enough to hold about 150 copies of the entire text and graphics for this book.

The personal computer was not the only new class of machines to emerge in the early 1980s. A first cousin to the PC was designed and bred for a different market, and it was to have a significant impact on the entire industry. A start-up company named Apollo Computer manufactured a desktop device called a *workstation*. Considerably more powerful than the PC, a workstation was originally intended for engineers and scientists who needed large computational capacity coupled with high-resolution computer graphics displays. Today, workstations and the software that runs on them represent a strategic business opportunity for every major computer company.

Mainframes, minicomputers, workstations, and PCs continue to be sold to a maturing computer market. In many cases, software has become the predominant contributor to profit, as competitive pressure has reduced profit margins for all classes of machines.

The Software Dilemma

It is difficult for any company to absorb these rapid developments economically and efficiently. Most large companies have an enormous investment—economic, cultural, and organizational—in mainframe computers and the software developed for them, typically developing ten million lines of code in support of their mainframes. Every year, as many as a million of the source lines are changed, removed, or added during the activity called *software maintenance*. When you consider that the average cost per line of code can easily exceed $25 (and sometimes reach $100 or more per line), the monetary investment is staggering.

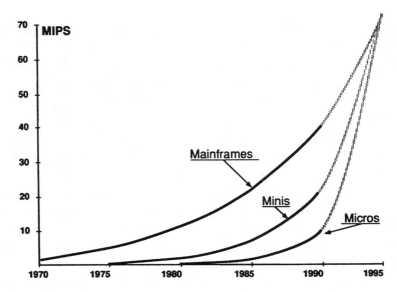

For the past twenty-five years, the power of all types of computers has increased at an ever-accelerating rate. Apparently, mainframe power for a fixed cost is accelerating less rapidly than minicomputing power, and microcomputing power is accelerating more rapidly than either of its older cousins. Experts disagree on the accuracy of these relative measurements and the classification of computing machines into such simple categories. However, one fact is clear: All classes of computers are increasing in power at a rate that will soon go off our current scales.

What of the workstations? In many cases, they have both the capacity and the facilities to outperform the mainframe for many information systems applications. Will major companies have to rewrite millions of lines of code to accommodate these new machines? Will they attempt to convert old programs to make them compatible with workstation technology? Will they do nothing, continuing to use the mainframe as the central computing resource, even as this technology becomes obsolete? None of these options is attractive, but every company will have to adopt one of them to survive the 1990s. Obviously, these companies cannot abandon support for their existing systems and jump immediately into the new technology. Conversely, they cannot maintain a competitive posture if they do not move toward the new technology and phase out the older systems. The kernel of this dilemma is not the hardware—decisions based on hardware alone are relatively simple. What makes the decision so difficult is software.

A recent article in the popular press summarized the workstation–software problem rather nicely:

> As desk-top computers have gotten more powerful, the software that goes with them has grown more complex, but writing software hasn't stepped up at all. It is done the old-fashioned way—one line of computer instructions at a time . . . at best software programmers create no more than 10 accurate lines a day. That's led to enormous delays in getting new programs done.[*]

Software must be built or purchased if mainframes, minicomputers, workstations, and PCs are to deliver on their promise. If the industry can do no better than ten accurate lines a day, the snowball may well shatter and its progress stop.

---

[*] "High Tech Blues," *USA Today*, July 7, 1989.

The Deadline

5
The Driving Force

Ed Riccio is Vice President of Technology Planning for a Fortune 100 company. "We just finished our Corporate Technology Study," he begins. "Every five years, we note those technologies that will have an impact on our business over the next decade. We examine the skill with which we're applying them. This time we identified twenty-four key technologies—materials science, fiber optics, telecommunications, genetic engineering—things like that.

"We noticed an interesting thing," muses Riccio. "Software is a leveraging technology for eighteen of the twenty-four entries on our list."

"What is a leveraging technology?" we ask.

"It gives us leverage," he explains. "Software is necessary to do the research and development needed to make practical use of the technology; it's necessary to build the manufacturing or process systems to transform raw technology into products; it's an integral part of many of the products that incorporate the technology."

"You mean it gives you the opportunity to exploit the technology for competitive advantage?" we ask.

"Yeah, that's it," says Riccio, "it opens up opportunity."

Software is the driving force behind most, if not all, modern technology because it is used at every stage in a technology's evolution. During the past three decades, software people have built a $300 billion industry of their own and have developed systems that support additional trillions of dollars in commerce. In the process, they have transformed much of the modern world.

Software is used to perform the initial scientific/engineering analysis and simulation required during the conception of a new technology and the transformation of the technology into a commercially viable product, system, or service. It is used to create the business plans necessary to determine the viability of the product in the marketplace. It often becomes part of the product, providing the "intelligence" that differentiates it from another. It is used to control manufacturing when the product is built and to track sales when the product is introduced to the marketplace. At every stage in the evolution of a technology, computer programs must be built, changed, or acquired. The information created by software drives progress toward the next stage.

Software's impact—its driving force—is not limited to technology alone. There are also behavioral, intellectual, and even sensory forces that are components of software. The user becomes the master of a complex computer-based system, but only because software is there to help. Without software, a neurosurgeon could not accurately position a probe to within a millimeter of diseased brain cells; a secretary could not generate six variations of the same basic letter in two minutes; an engineer could not build a three-dimensional model of a new automobile and "drive" it through a simulated wind tunnel without ever leaving his desk; a child could not command a video game spacecraft that battles with an alien armada. All of these users modify their behavior to adapt to a complex system. They all experience a magnification of their skills. They all react to sensory stimuli that are generated by a computer program.

For example, a neurosurgeon positions a probe by observing its movement through an electronic representation of the brain—an image displayed on a color monitor, collected from data gathered from sophisticated X-ray scanners. The probe position is controlled by a robot arm that receives commands from the surgeon. Software is responsible for the images that direct the neurosurgeon, as well as for executing his or her commands.

In Chapter 1, we referred to software as an information composite—it is information, it uses information, and it creates information. This information is synthesized in a way that creates a virtual world for the user. Software offers the opportunity to accumulate and exploit information. It is essential because we now create systems that are too complex to be controlled without computers. We require automation, and automation requires software.

An example of one such mammoth, highly complex computer project is the U.S. Defense Department's Strategic Defense Initiative (SDI). SDI has been estimated to require between 30 and 50 million lines of code and cost between $30 and $50 *billion* to develop. The summary on the following page of the sorts of numbers being contemplated can give a quick idea of the huge impact this one software project is expected to have.

Danger Signs

In the 1950s and 1960s, many observers criticized the steel industry in the United States for lack of investment in its physical plant. Over time, factories deteriorated; modern methods were nonexistent; quality and productivity suffered. As a result, steel prices climbed, and the domestic steel industry suffered, losing significant market share to foreign competition—competition that had newer plants with more advanced technology, that instituted a primary focus on product quality, and that was provided with government subsidies to make them extremely cost-competitive.

During that period, many people in the fledgling computer industry regarded the steel industry with contempt. "If they're unwilling to invest in their own business," software people remarked, "they deserve to lose market share." Those words may well come back to haunt the software world.

Estimated Costs of Very Large Software Projects

During the next decade, large corporations and government agencies will embark on very large software projects. The costs of such projects and the risks associated with them boggle the mind.

Consider the Strategic Defense Initiative using data already collected for the Space Shuttle project

Space Shuttle Software:

    size: 500,000 lines of code (LOC)
    cost: $1,000 per LOC
    quality: 0.1 defect / KLOC (1,000 LOC)
    changes: 4,000 changes over 5 years
    tools: 2 million LOC to support 500,000 LOC of mission software

SDI Software:

    size estimate: 30 million - 50 million LOC

Using data from the space shuttle, we can project the following costs and risks:

    Total cost: $30 billion - $50 billion
    quality: (@ 0.1 defects/KLOC) **300,000 - 500,000 defects**
    changes:
        40,000 changes over 5 years
        8,000 per year
        30 changes per day
        (all have to be controlled and tested)
    cost of change:
        assume each change modifies 100 LOC
        assume cost to modify each line is twice the cost to create
        therefore, each change costs $200,000
        yearly cost for software support: $1.6 billion
    tools:
        using same ratio as space shuttle: 200 million LOC
        cost for support tools: $20 billion

Some of the expected costs and effort for SDI, based on related data from the space shuttle project.

The software industry in the United States today is in a position quite similar to the steel industry's of the 1950s and 1960s. Across companies and organizations large and small, there is an aging software plant with thousands of critical software-based applications in dramatic need of refurbishing. Yet managers at these companies are unwilling or unable to commit the resources for this work. "Just patch the problems," they say, "and we'll worry about rebuilding it next year."

It will not be enough to "patch" what's broken. Many components of the software plant require significant re-engineering, or the companies that use them will not be competitive in the 1990s and beyond.

Many might argue that the preceding metaphor is weak, since the steel industry faced competition from Europe and Asia. Where will the competition for the software industry come from?

The fact is that competition for software supremacy is forming right now. It will be intense, it will be competent, and it will be here sooner than many think. Japan, Singapore, Korea, Taiwan, India, China, and many other nations (including countries in western and eastern Europe) offer a large pool of highly motivated, competently educated, and relatively low-cost computer professionals. This work force is moving rapidly to adopt state-of-the-art software engineering methods and tools and may very well become a force to be reckoned with during the 1990s.

Competition in the Land of the Rising Sun

In the Far East, Japan has already established a world-class software development capability. The Japanese established their first "software factory"—the Hitachi Software Works—in the late 1960s. Unlike their American counterparts, Japanese software developers have focused on *software process improvement,* rather than *software product innovation.* In the short term, a focus on product innovation has enabled the United States to dominate the software market. But in the long term, the results may be different. Japanese software engineers measure; they tune, they standardize, they build better tools—all in an effort to improve the software development process and, as a result, build high-quality, reliable products. As we will see in Chapter 8, it is the *process* that leaves a legacy for future generations of software developers. It may be the emphasis on process improvement that will ultimately provide the Japanese with leadership in software.

Japan is not the only competition. Singapore has established a national information technology strategy to develop a software service industry. The government of Singapore has instituted financial incentives to attract overseas technology leaders to establish software development centers in Singapore and to develop its own software technology industry.* Although these initial efforts are small (minuscule by U.S. standards), the rate of growth is significant. In 1980, there were approximately 850 software development professionals in all of Singapore. Today, there are more than 8,000 software engineers in that country. In contrast, the number of college freshmen enrolled in computer and software-related majors in the United States has decreased every year since 1987.

Some American companies have already thrown in the towel and begun *outsourcing,* whereby a company severely cuts its information systems staff and contracts all new software development, much of its ongoing systems maintenance, and all of its computer operations to a third party. Unknown to most people in the software world a few years ago, outsourcing may become common practice during the next decade. To date, outsourcing is conducted in conjunction with local service bureaus, but because this trend has one primary goal—to save money—it won't be long before outsourcing goes off-shore. If an American-based service bureau can do the work for x, an off-shore competitor can likely do the same work

---

*T.J. Chin and K.Y. Wong, "Software Technology Development in Singapore," *IEEE Software,* Vol. 6, No. 2 (March 1989), pp. 61-65.

for y, where y is much less than x. Recall that in the 1960s, RCA and Motorola attempted to cut television costs by outsourcing only a few electronic components to off-shore manufacturers. The core industry would remain in the U.S., they said. Today, there are no major consumer electronics manufacturers left in the United States. An entire industry migrated off-shore. Could this happen to the software industry, too?

Maybe this isn't a problem. Foreign competition has already eliminated the U.S. home electronics industry and drastically reduced market share in the automotive, machine tool, and industrial electronics sectors. But in each of these markets, consumers have access to high-quality products at reduced cost. Won't this happen for software as well? If history is our guide, perhaps we as software consumers should aggressively push toward outsourcing.

The problem in such action lies in the very nature and power of software. Does software exist outside the computer that executes it? If so, what does it represent? When removed from a machine, software is no longer simply computer programs. Software becomes a repository for collective knowledge.

Of Knowledge and Power

In their book on the impact of information services on the U.S. and the world, Feigenbaum and McCorduck state:

> Knowledge is power, and the computer is an amplifier of that power.... The American computer industry has been innovative, vital, and successful. It is, in a way, the ideal industry. It creates value by transforming the brainpower of the knowledge workers, with little consumption of energy and raw materials. Today, we dominate the world's ideas and markets in this most important of all modern technologies. But what about tomorrow?[*]

---

[*]E.A. Feigenbaum and P. McCorduck, *The Fifth Generation: Artificial Intelligence and Japan's Computer Challenge to the World* (Reading, Mass.: Addison-Wesley, 1983), p. 1.

Indeed, what about tomorrow? Computer hardware has already become a commodity, available from many sources. Yet software remains an industry where the U.S. has been "innovative, vital, and successful." Will we maintain our place at the top?

Feigenbaum and McCorduck may be closer to the mark than many of us want to believe. There are economic, political, technological, and national security reasons why the United States cannot afford to lose its leadership in software development technologies. Yet we do nothing about our aging software plant. There may come a time when it will be less costly to outsource software development and maintenance to third parties located halfway around the world. These third parties will be competent, supported by their government, and therefore very competitive. Software is not steel, but foreign competition may make them look very much alike.

The software industry in the United States must ask itself, Is it creativity or execution that leads to continuing dominance in a world market? The history of manufacturing suggests that execution (improving the process through which a product is built, thereby reducing cost and increasing quality) is key to long-term market dominance. Without an aggressive effort to fix the aging software plant— to re-engineer aging programs, to improve the process through which we build new software, to invest in tools, to educate and motivate software professionals—our creative edge in software will not sustain us for long.

Computing Power: Potential and Reality

From the earliest days, we had powerful computers, sitting there just waiting to do our bidding. The potential was obvious, but to tap it, we needed computer programs, which took months and often years to develop. It didn't take very long to recognize that with all of its empowering characteristics, software was also a bottleneck. It was frustrating to know that a problem could be solved algorithmically, that the data were available, that the program to couple the algorithm and the data was doable, and then to have to wait a week, a month, even a year or two to gain the benefits that were so obvious right now.

The computing community was resource-limited. Although the number of programmers increased, they couldn't keep pace with the ever-growing demand for new programs. To deal with the backlog, people at first talked about solving a *software problem.* "All we need is better programming languages, more memory, and faster computers," they said.

New languages were introduced, more memory was made available, and machines got much faster, but the software problem remained. Something had to be done, and in an attempt to dramatize the problem, the phrase *software crisis* was coined during the late 1960s.

There is a certain irony in the choice of that particular term. "Crisis" is defined in *Webster's Dictionary* as "a turning point in the course of anything; a decisive or crucial time, stage or event." Yet, for software there has been no turning point, no decisive time, only slow, evolutionary change. In the software industry, a crisis has existed for close to thirty years, and that is a contradiction in terms.

At a recent conference in Geneva, Switzerland, author and software methodologist Daniel Teichroew suggested that the real nature of the software industry's problems points more toward a chronic affliction: An affliction, he explained, is "anything causing pain or distress," and "chronic" means "lasting a long time or recurring often; continuing indefinitely."

There is no miracle prescription to make the affliction disappear, but there are many ways to reduce the pain as the search for a cure continues. In Part III, we'll examine the people whose charter is to find the cure.

Part III
Culture, Community, and Creation

As we mature, we progress though a series of passages. In her book of the same name, Gail Sheehy describes the growth process like this:

> We have been taught that children develop by ages and stages, that the steps are pretty much the same for everybody, and that to grow out of the limited behavior of childhood we must climb them all. Children alternate between stages of equilibrium and disequilibrium. As parents, we are educated not to blame these extremes of behavior on a teacher, the other parent, or the children themselves, but to accept them as the essential steps to growth.[*]

A technology and the people involved with it go through a similar series of passages as the technology matures. Much like children, they move quickly through stages of equilibrium and disequilibrium, falling down and rising to walk another step. The steps are pretty much the same for every company and every software technologist, and in order to mature, everyone involved must climb them all.

In the chapters that follow, we'll examine three components of the passages experienced by software organizations: the software culture that has spawned the tremendous creativity and accomplishments of the field; the people who form the software community—the skills, roles, and perspectives of the many groups who make software happen; and the creative process—the concepts, tools, and techniques that define software technology.

---

[*]G. Sheehy, *Passages: Predictable Crises of Adult Life* (New York: E.P. Dutton, 1976), p. 11.

The Game Board

6
Corporate Cultures

The image is classic 1980s Americana: Two twenty-three-year-old college dropouts decide they have a great idea for a computer program. Using money they saved while working at a Burger King, they buy a personal computer and start a software company in their garage.

After working day and night for months, they create a program that becomes a ubiquitous tool of thousands of businesses around the world. They become multimillionaires by (a) selling the company to a large conglomerate; (b) being bought out by the venture capitalists who funded the company's expansion, or (c) sticking with the company, molding it in their image, and creating a major software vendor listed on the New York Stock Exchange.

And they live happily ever after.

It should come as no surprise that for every two people who have succeeded in building a software company, thousands have failed. In fact, the golden age of out-of-the-garage software companies is already behind us. For reasons that we will consider in this chapter, two guys in a garage stand very little chance of succeeding in the software business of the 1990s and beyond.

This is a chapter about corporate cultures, and the start-up form is only one of many. Today, many established companies have multiple hundred million dollar divisions that are software companies. Other medium-size Fortune 1000 companies (some that actually were started in garages) have made their mark in the software business and are now diversifying. Finally, there are the hundreds of small software companies, many of which have been starting up for almost a decade.

The Establishment

The twenty-year plaque on Mike Stratten's corner office wall is displayed with pride. Stratten has paid his dues, starting as a junior hardware engineer and progressing through the ranks of one of the largest multinational corporations on earth. He's spent time in the Midwest working in aerospace, in the East on factory automation, and in the West managing engineering product development for military applications. Today, he is Vice President of Engineering for a division of a company that makes state-of-the-art medical equipment. He has 245 people working for him. One hundred and sixty of them are software engineers.

"We're very traditional in our approach to engineering," says Stratten. "After all, we've been around for a very long time and we have an entrenched culture.

"Most of us think of ourselves as a hardware company—we make things for consumers, for industry, for governments. Look at this division. We make CAT scanners and magnetic imaging systems, as well as specialized radiographic devices. It's a pretty impressive piece of hardware."

Stratten stares out the window, contemplating changes to his world. "It's difficult for me to adapt to the fact that I now have more software engineers than hardware engineers. That we're spending more money building computer programs than we spend engineering hardware. I came up through the ranks when software was a service function for engineering—now it's becoming engineering in this division. Sometimes I get the feeling that the tail's wagging the dog."

Mike Stratten, like thousands of other senior managers in established technology companies, is seeing the world of engineering gravitate toward software. New products often have very little new hardware, but they may have new or improved software that provides better features, functionality, or performance. These features enable companies to reach new customers and expand market share. Software is often the competitive edge.

Despite its importance, many established technology companies don't really understand software. Most recognize that changes are occurring and grudgingly accept them, but they continue to manage their companies as if software remained a support function. Mike Stratten's division and many like it are rapidly becoming software companies, yet no one really wants to admit it. After all, established companies like General Electric, Exxon, or Kodak can trace their history back to the start of the century—long before software or computers existed—yet they now all have major software divisions.

Because managers of some old-line companies didn't grow up in the software business, they often treat software development like a stepchild. Software developers can sense this—especially if expenditures on tools, training, and hiring are inadequate or career paths in software dead-end.

Of course, there are many other technology companies that have embraced software engineering as the pivotal technology for success in the 1990s and beyond. These tend to be either younger companies or older companies that have created high-technology businesses over the past three decades.

Surprisingly, in certain nontechnology market sectors, software has been more rapidly integrated into the fabric of the main business and been more readily accepted by senior management. Banks and insurance companies, for example, as well as many other large service corporations have created a new executive—the chief information officer (CIO)—as the czar of computing with ultimate responsibility for software development throughout the corporation. These companies have recognized software's strategic importance in manufacturing, engineering, accounting, inventory, market analysis, training, personal productivity, and many other areas.

The Young Bulls

There's a bawdy parable that does much to explain the relationship between the young bulls—technology companies that have seen enormous growth over the past two decades—and older establishment companies:

> As the last of the Winter snows were melting, two bulls stood on a hilltop eating grass and surveying the green pastures and rolling hills that surrounded them. One of the bulls had seen many Springs; the other had just reached maturity.
> Suddenly the young bull jerked his head. "Hey," he said to his older compatriot, "look at those cows down there in the valley. Some of them are pretty cute."
> The older bull glanced up, grunted his agreement, and went back to munching on the grass at his feet.
> The young bull stopped eating entirely and focused on the herd of cows. "I've got an idea," said the younger one. "Why don't we run down the hill and make love to two of those cows?"
> "I've got a better idea," said the older bull. "Why don't we *walk* down the hill and make love to *all* of them."

Companies that we characterize as "the young bulls" are much like their namesake in our parable. They are aggressive, full of their own success, and focused on one technology or product line.* Some are relatively small, having revenues between $20 and $100 million, while others have ascended to the Fortune 500. All make use of software in the products, systems, and services that are pivotal to their business, and their software culture is often radically different from established companies.

Because they are younger companies, their culture accommodates software with little upheaval. Senior managers are nearly always computer- and software-literate. All of them have worked with software people throughout their careers and many have spent time writing programs. Some—even those who have reached senior levels—still view themselves as technical hotshots in software or a related discipline.

Now, you might think that software people in young bull companies are nurtured and coddled like a firstborn. After all, management has been there, they understand. But management also understands something else—aggressive product development. Time is the single commodity that is in short supply and, sadly, time is the key needed to produce a high-quality product. Employee burnout is a natural consequence of the pressured environment of a young bull company.

> Sheila McMartin is one of four software development managers for a computer manufacturer that has experienced forty percent annual growth for the past five years. The thirty-six people who work for McMartin build systems software. To say Sheila is harried is to be a master of understatement.
>
> "I haven't worked an eight-hour day since I got here four years ago," McMartin states. There's a fierce pride in her eyes—statements like this are the macho creed for software managers in young bull companies.

---

*We have encountered a few young bulls that would say, "Okay, I've got an even better idea. Let's *run* down the hill and make love to all of them— *twice.*"

"Aren't you worried about burnout?" we ask.

Sheila laughs. "I'm not burnt out—I'm incinerated. But the work is really challenging, I'm given free reign to get the job done, I've got good people, and I get respect (when we get the product out the door). I wouldn't have it any other way."

The deliver-on-time-at-any-cost creed—a philosophy that permeates almost every young bull company—leaves little time for anything else. Staff members and managers are given free reign to create, but cleaning up the mess afterward can be painful.

Young bull companies grow so fast that they have little time for the kind of discipline and controls that lead to high-quality software engineering. More and more software keeps leaving the loading dock, more and more customers sign on, more and more pressure is levied to create the next version, the next generation, the next home run. Unfortunately, more and more also means increased demand for customer support, error correction, and customized enhancements—things that become an expensive burden as the young bull matures. If the software produced as the young bull matures is sloppily designed and hurriedly implemented, the company will often hit the wall.

Customer support and software maintenance costs that may have been increasing at a leisurely three-to-five percent a year can accelerate dramatically. Resources that the young bull once used to build new products must be dedicated to the care and feeding of the existing line of software-based products. Adaptations, corrections, and enhancements are difficult to make because there was little planning for them while the software was being built. Progress slows, customers moan, management screams—but the die has been cast. The young bull's cavalier attitude toward software turns a dream into a nightmare. Software was once the engine of the young bull company. Now, it is the brakes.

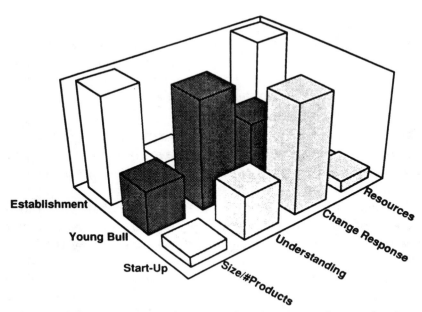

Comparison of types of companies in the software business: Those companies with the resources to support new product development are hampered by their inability to respond to changes in the environment.

The Start-Up

As we noted earlier, the start-up is a quintessentially American phenomenon and no industry has made it easier to start up than the software industry. A survey of the American populace would probably show that a large percentage of us has at some time considered starting a business. The appeal of this idea is the control of our own destiny and the possibility of financial independence, not to mention the easy commute to work if the business is home-based.

However, this dream begins to fade when we realize the substantial risk involved in any independent venture—space must be rented, inventory and equipment acquired, people hired to do at least some of the work, accountants and lawyers retained . . . the list is quite long. Worse, the list (and associated costs) can grow even longer if the new venture is in a technology area.

For example, say you decide to start a company to build electric automobiles. Environmental concerns look promising for opening the market in the twenty-first century. You'll need engineers, a manufacturing plant, and a large staff of marketing and administrative workers, just to get started. The price of opening the door can easily be tens of millions of dollars. And once the prototype product is built, you'll need to establish an elaborate distribution network to ship, sell, and service the automobile. Even if you can finance all of this, you will then have to contend with a crushing load of government regulations and ferocious competition from long-established companies. If you don't think this will be tough, ask John DeLorean.

Now, suppose you want to start a company to build a software product for personal computers. To begin, you take over the family room in your home.* The equipment you will need consists of a personal computer, a modem, and a telephone; these and any furniture can probably be acquired for less than $10,000. You'll need to know how to program (or you'll have to take on a partner who does), and you'll need an innovative idea (more on this later). After months or years of dedicated effort, your product is ready.

Manufacturing is easy: Put a blank disk in the computer and in a few seconds, you have a copy of the product. Sure, you'll have to pay a few bucks for packaging and someone will have to put the user's manual into readable form, but none of that is particularly expensive or difficult. You now have a company and a product, but you probably haven't yet made a dime. Now the hard part begins.

In the early 1980s, the market for personal computer software was wide open. The scarcity of useful programs meant that any

---

*Although the garage shop is a romantic notion, the smell of gasoline and the click of a personal computer keyboard don't peacefully coexist. Besides, a month's work can be run over by a sixteen-year-old with a learner's permit.

good new idea could be presented to the marketplace at relatively low cost and distributed by an array of eager sales outlets. Every personal computer software company was small and inexperienced, so competition was on an equal footing.

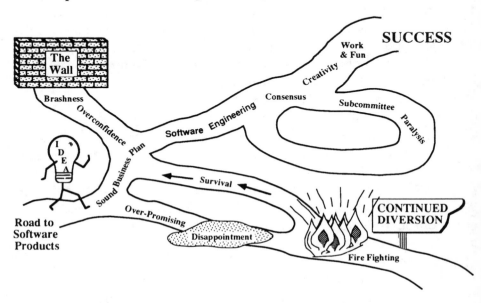

An idea will encounter many passages on the road to becoming a successful software product.

Today, the market for personal computer software is saturated. New products must fight for expensive advertising space and distribution outlets. A newcomer must compete with the likes of Borland, Lotus, or Microsoft, former young bulls that evolved from start-up to giant during the 1980s. Competition is fierce and even good ideas often die before they reach a broad market. (We don't mean to discourage you budding software entrepreneurs, but it is best to enter the business with your eyes wide open.)

A software start-up might actually have better luck today concentrating on products for more powerful platforms such as workstations or mainframes. Start-up costs are somewhat greater (you can always rent computer time), but software is not a capital-intensive business. Competition will be equally intense, but the opportunity for a good idea is always open.

It's Crazy, But It Just Might Work

In the late 1930s and early 1940s, Mickey Rooney and Judy Garland starred in a series of movies with virtually identical story lines: A group of kids were faced with adversity (usually economic). One of them came up with an idea (usually putting on a talent show) to overcome the adversity. Adults thought of a hundred reasons why it wouldn't work (and often forbade it). But one of the stars (usually Judy Garland) would invariably say, "It's crazy, but it just might work." With that, success and happiness were merely a reel or two away.

Although the scenario is somewhat different, many software entrepreneurs have pursued their own it's-crazy-but-it-just-might-work ideas. A truly new idea is rare indeed, and most "new" ideas are actually adaptations of existing concepts or a repackaging of an old approach. Computer-based spreadsheets, desktop publishing, and personal money management programs are some examples of adaptations of existing concepts and approaches that were new to the computing marketplace.

In many cases, the company that originates a new idea will have mixed success. After educating the market on the underlying concept, selling the customer on the need for the concept, and making a tidy profit because of its uniqueness in the marketplace, the originator is often leapfrogged by a competitor that produces a similar product, but with features that the market defines after using the originator's product.

The classic example of this situation is the history of the spreadsheet program. The players: Visicorp (now defunct), Lotus Development Corporation, and Microsoft. In the early days of personal computing, Visicorp pioneered the spreadsheet idea and turned Visicalc into the hottest selling software product of its time. But Visicalc was a bare bones spreadsheet and the company, flush with success (and possibly suffering with a program that was not easy to adapt), did not respond to the market's demands for improved ease of use and more sophisticated functions. After Visicorp blazed the trail by demonstrating market demand, Lotus Development, an aggressive and well-funded start-up, introduced Lotus 1-2-3®. With much advertising fanfare, the company claimed that 1-2-3 did everything that Visicalc did and did it better. The market agreed and within some eighteen months, Lotus 1-2-3 became the world's most widely used spreadsheet program. And Visicorp ... well, they were eventually purchased by Lotus and disappeared.

Lotus was the king of the IBM PC, but in the late 1980s, the Apple Macintosh gained momentum. Lotus found that its software was not easily adaptable to the Macintosh. Recognizing an opportunity, Microsoft improved on Lotus's work and introduced Excel® and soon captured market share for Macintosh spreadsheets.

Similar stories have occurred in software applications areas that range from computer-aided design to accounting, from automated manufacturing to video games, from database management to inventory control, from project planning to hospital administration. In the software business, being first is not always an advantage.

Everybody Else Is Stupid

All companies, young and old, large and small, can be afflicted by brashness and/or overconfidence. Large companies have often achieved some level of success and stability in their internal software needs. Confident in their success, management may assume that past decisions regarding information systems technology will continue to be valid in the future.

Young bulls and start-ups can also suffer from brashness and overconfidence. If the company has one success or generates a unique idea, personnel will understandably be proud and feel an exhilaration, akin to beating a difficult opponent in a sporting event. Since managers (usually the founders) and technical people have succeeded where others have failed, they may begin to feel "everybody else is stupid." Sadly, many software companies that take this attitude win the battle but lose the war.

Jerry Ashton is the forty-year-old CEO of a software company that builds programs for the banking industry. In 1982, Jerry left a Big Eight accounting firm, spent $400 to incorporate a new company, and devoted the next six months to writing a program in a specialized area of financial management. It caught on, and Jerry's company grew.

"In those days, our sales were doubling every year," reminisces Ashton. "We grew to eighteen people and I was doing most of the managing and most of the programming. Damn, we were hot!

"Today, we're just under a hundred people, growing at almost forty percent per year," says Jerry. "We do things my way. After all, you can't argue with success.

"We have two-dozen software developers and sometimes I'd like to get rid of them all," laments Jerry. "It takes forever to get a change made. Something that would take me five minutes to do takes one of them all day."

Jerry Ashton insists on being involved in every technical decision for all seven of the company's products. He has become a bottleneck. Worse, he insists the old ways of programming are best and thinks companies that do software engineering are stupid for wasting their time.

What Jerry doesn't realize is that everyone else isn't stupid. The reason it takes his people all day to make a simple change is that they must struggle with the poorly constructed program architecture that he built. Yet he insists his way is best. After all, who can argue with success?

The Wall

Jerry Ashton's company, and many others that are far bigger, are headed for the wall—a time when brashness and overconfidence come home to roost, when old technology cannot be further patched and pushed, when revenues drop and problems take over. The wall approaches because companies refuse to recognize that they must change. The wall looms because a company's decision makers don't stay abreast of technology changes, assume a small competitor cannot apply sufficient resources to compete and a large competitor cannot match its own creativity, and stick to the old ways even when their competitors have abandoned similar approaches.

With all these warnings about overconfidence, a young company can easily become discouraged. Success in the software business does not come to the faint of heart; companies must adapt to changing times, and they must move ahead. Industry giants like IBM and AT&T have fought the everybody-else-is-stupid syndrome and won (more than they've lost), with such products as the legendary PC and the ubiquitous UNIX® operating system. Other brash companies—Sun Microsystems, Apple Computer, Microsoft, Lotus Development—all have proved they can play with the establishment and win.

One of the many legends of California's Silicon Valley and Boston's Route 128 concerns a software company that experienced enormous success in a very short time. The company's management encouraged outrageous thinking, and to reinforce their out-of-the-mainstream style, they floated a rubber duck in the fountain at their corporate headquarters. As the company grew larger and even more successful and powerful, a new management team emerged. The rubber duck disappeared from the corporate fountain (it wasn't seemly for a major technology company to be so frivolous). Gradually, the company's most creative people went the way of the duck, and so did the creative edge that had made it so successful.

Our message to all software companies both large and small is, *"If you don't have a rubber duck, get one. If you already have a rubber duck, don't give it a seat on the board of directors."*

Consensus and Paralysis

In order for a software organization to succeed and prosper, a primary goal must be to get the most from each employee. One of the best ways to do this is through a technique known as *management by consensus.* This technique borrows from the principles of democratic government and suggests that because employees control their own destiny, higher performance and a sense of dedication to the corporate goals results. Senior management sets the broad strategies and directions for the corporation and then leaves employees the freedom to develop their own plans and goals to achieve company objectives. This is usually done through group decision making.

Group decision making is a double-edged sword, however. It can lead to creative thinking (certainly in the software business, two brains are better than one). But as a technology company grows from young bull to establishment, it can also lead to paralysis. A variation—subcommittee paralysis—goes something like this:

A problem has come to the attention of a company's senior management, who appoint a committee of technical managers to find a solution. The committee decides the problem is too large, breaks it into smaller, more manageable pieces, and creates a subcommittee to study each one. Subcommittees A, B, and C are made up of some members of the original committee, plus personnel with expertise related to the specific task of each subcommittee. The subcommittees meet, conclude they have insufficient technical information to address the problem, and consequently commission several study groups composed of technical experts to acquire and supply the necessary background for sound decision making. The technical groups are now three levels removed from the original problem definition and hence spend an enormous amount of energy trying to ascertain why they are pursuing the task they have been given. Because all of the technical study groups are working toward a common goal (the solution of the original problem), they will inevitably cross paths in their search for information. Often this leads to group conflict, confusion, and infighting. Once this begins, it can so delay the decision making process that in the fast-moving world of high-technology systems and products, the original problem may have evolved into something entirely different before the first answer can be achieved.

Subcommittee paralysis can be avoided if the original committee remains lean and focused and if the members can get the necessary technical information quickly through an advisory group of experts. These technical experts are sometimes referred to as "gatekeepers," after the ancient gatekeepers of a walled city or castle. A technological gatekeeper must provide information on the comings and goings in a particular technical world outside the company's walls. Gatekeepers should be experienced individuals who understand both the technology and the business of the company.

Work and Fun

It was one of those awkward campus get-togethers. An alumnus, now very successful, was mingling with faculty and students after an awards ceremony and speech. He was an entrepreneur's entrepreneur, founding four companies before he was 42 years old. Each had made its mark, and each had made him very wealthy (hence, the campus award!).

A young engineering student gathered her courage and approached the entrepreneur.

"I read the description of your career and I'm amazed," said the student in point-blank style. "How did you become so successful? How do I do what you did?"

The entrepreneur smiled (having heard the same question three times in the previous forty minutes), "What do you mean by successful?" he asked.

After a moment's hesitation, the student responded, "I guess to do what you want to do and make a lot of money doing it."

"There's only one answer," said the entrepreneur, "Have fun."

"Have fun?"

"Yep, it's the only way you'll stay interested long enough to have a chance at being successful."

Sage advice, and often forgotten. One of the reasons software people work long hours, suffer enormous pressure, put up with unsympathetic customers, and still produce high-quality products is because they enjoy the work—they have fun. Their prime motivation is meeting the challenge that the technology offers, and their greatest satisfaction is seeing their efforts solve a problem that others could not. In his book that explores the beginnings of the computer revolution, Steven Levy writes:

> As I talked to these digital explorers, ranging from those who tamed multimillion-dollar machines in the 1950s to contemporary young wizards who mastered computers in their suburban bedrooms, I found a common element, a common philosophy which . . . was a philosophy of sharing, openness, decentralization, and getting your hands on machines at any cost—to improve the machines, and to improve the world.[*]

Sadly, as a company grows, the associated bureaucracy sometimes dampens the fun factor. Technical managers and practitioners either leave, or lose the fun and work less effectively, or become guerrilla fighters and have fun in spite of their environment.

---

[*]S. Levy, *Hackers: Heroes of the Computer Revolution* (Garden City, N.Y.: Anchor Press/Doubleday, 1984), p. 1.

Structure in the Midst of Chaos

In our discussion of corporate software cultures, we have purposely spent little time considering what would traditionally be called corporate structure. In start-up companies, there is little formal structure—everybody is responsible for everything—but this must change as the number of people doing software grows.

An organizational chart for a typical software developer usually contains (or should contain) six organizational units. Yet, in many companies only two—software engineering and software maintenance—are formally organized. The other four functions are ignored structurally, even though they can't be ignored in reality. Somebody has to do research, customers must be dealt with, engineering must be done at the systems level, and the entire process must be managed and coordinated. To do the work, staff members in engineering or maintenance carry the extra burden of these activities. The problem is that this extra burden dilutes the work that they are able to perform in their primary area of responsibility. Over time and with growth, the following functional units become formalized in most software organizations:

Product research monitors the work of competing companies and studies technological advances in the industry. In many ways, the role of product research should be as a technology transfer agent; that is, the product research group studies a new technology to understand local applications for it. It is here that prototyping and feasibility studies are done, and it is the home of the gatekeeper.

Software engineering includes people who analyze, design, implement, and test software. The priorities and specifications for new applications are developed through cooperation with the customer support and product research groups. Often, the techies in this group do a tour of duty with the customer support group so they can maintain contact with the end user. This is the domain of the sorcerer and apprentices, people whom we'll discuss in Chapter 7.

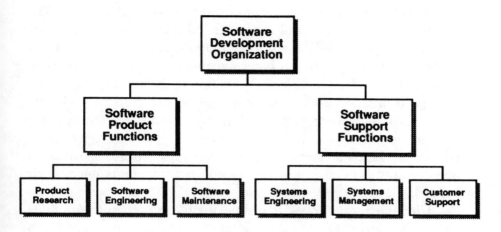

Organizational chart for a typical software company.

Software maintenance is responsible for error correction and minor adaptations and enhancements. In most cases, the customer support group gives the maintenance group its marching orders. This is where the fire fighters live.*

Systems engineering is the link between the software and the hardware. For pure software organizations, this group is often called the systems group and is responsible for the development of systems software (including the operating systems, utilities, and tools). For a company that delivers *turnkey systems* (those with integrated hardware and software solutions) or *embedded products* (that is, products with software intelligence), the engineering development group performs the analysis and design necessary to integrate hardware components with the software.

---

*If a company delivers a product plagued with errors and design flaws, it must resort to fire fighting to deal with emergencies. Unfortunately, software fire fighting can become a way of life in some start-ups. And if all of the resources become involved in dealing with emergencies, an organization will never be able to develop sound reliable products.

Systems management is the catchall name for the group that performs those tasks that nobody else is willing or able to do. The group controls the library of programs and documentation and handles the integration of the work done by the separate development and maintenance groups. It is responsible for packaging and shipping software releases, as well as cataloging and accounting for error reports produced by the customer support group and fixed by the software maintenance group. In many companies, the systems management group is also responsible for computer operations, overseeing hardware repair, making backups, installing software updates, and generally policing all computer systems under their control.

Customer support is the most visible group to the outside world. In many cases, the only direct contact a customer has with a software company is through a hot line monitored by customer support. That's why the competence and interpersonal skills of the customer support staff can often affect the success or failure of a product. If the voice at the other end of the phone is knowledgeable, competent, and courteous, the customer will react favorably even if the program is flawed. Companies with a reputation for solid customer service rarely fail.

The activities of each of the six organizational units discussed above would be suspect without a *software quality assurance* (SQA) group to ensure that all software built and maintained within the company has high quality (see Chapter 8). So why have we not shown SQA on the organizational chart? Simply because SQA must be *independent* so that it is not influenced by delivery deadlines, budgetary issues, or local politics. It should report to a higher level of management or to the marketing organization but never to the sales department.

The Last Word on Corporate Cultures

If there's only one thing we've learned in our years in the software business, it's that every company has its own culture and that cultures evolve. The culture of a software organization changes as the size of the company changes, as the products change, as the people change, and as attitudes change. It is transformed to accommodate greater control and then is modified to relax control. Culture is always in a state of flux.

A good manager finds the essence of a company and attempts to preserve it even as culture changes. If the company has become successful by allowing a freewheeling, creative style with ducks in the fountain, this style should not be lost, even as the company grows and the culture evolves.

The Proof

7
Who Are the People?

In the early days of computing, programmers were viewed as the strangers in the back room. Few people really understood what they did and fewer cared to find out. Yet, one thing was obvious. These "strangers" were quite unlike their colleagues who worked in the front office. Front office people worked normal business hours. Programmers often came into work at 3:00 P.M., worked until 3:00 A.M., then left for two days only to return and work thirty-six hours straight.

The front office folks had degrees in conventional fields of study—marketing, finance, accounting, engineering, even physics, chemistry, or math. Some of the strangers had degrees that appeared to have no relationship to the work that they did—degrees in English literature, psychology, or music. Others migrated from the fields of science, engineering, or business and were now computer types. A few were trained in a new discipline that was even more mysterious—computer science.

Front office people dressed alike and spoke a language that was understandable to all of their peers. From the very beginning, programmers wore jeans and a flannel shirt, when a jacket and tie were viewed as *de rigueur.* They spoke the arcane language of computing, peppering every sentence with terms such as "asynchronous multiprocessing," "nibbles," or "IEEE 488 interfacing protocol."

In the early days of computing, the general public understood so little about computers and programming that the role of a programmer was viewed as just another obscure technical activity, akin to an entomologist or a lapidary. Today, people understand more about computers, and popular, but incorrect, images of programmers and software engineers have become embedded in the public consciousness. On the one hand, people who program computers are viewed as nerds—one-dimensional techies who have no personality, no interests outside of a computer keyboard, few interpersonal skills, and virtually no panache. On the other hand, software people are sometimes characterized as hackers—modern-day information pirates whose skill and creativity enable them to travel the communication pathways of the world, breaking into business and government computers in a never-ending pursuit of fun. Both of these stereotypes are so popular that successful motion pictures were made about each during the 1980s. (*Revenge of the Nerds* celebrated the first stereotype, and *War Games* depicted the second.)

Like many stereotypes, there are elements of truth in these characterizations, but they represent extreme ends of a spectrum. In this chapter, we'll examine the middle of the spectrum and the people who reside there—the real players in the software game.

A Personality Profile

There are countless studies that address the question, What set of traits defines a good programmer or software person? Like any collection of research that delves into roles that people play, the results, although interesting, have been inconclusive. One software manager we know uses a very simple criterion for selecting potential job candidates.

"I ask whether they're interested in music," he says. "In my experience, the best programmers enjoy the classics—Bach or Mozart. I think it has something to do with an appreciation of structure as an art form. But I'm finding fewer and fewer new grads who fit my profile," he admits with a smile. "Maybe it's time to find something new."

He doesn't use a love of classical music as his only criterion, but it plays a major role in his decision. The software projects that he manages are rarely late and almost always above average in technical quality, and his people are among the best contributors in the information systems department. Who can argue with success?

Many companies give detailed aptitude tests to isolate those individuals who show the potential for becoming good software developers. One of the best ones we know flunked a programming aptitude test early in her career, but is now a bright star in the arcane world of operating systems engineering.

So what is the personality profile? People who do a good job of developing software often have an unusual and sometimes contradictory mix of personality traits and technical skills:

- They are *creative*. Software developers often begin with a blank sheet of paper and create a program that solves some complex problem.

- They are *obsessive*. When a problem is encountered, software developers must be willing to dedicate all of their energies to a small area of a program that isn't functioning, working tirelessly until it's fixed.

- They are *intuitive*. There are times when intuition (others might call this association or cognitive skill) will lead software developers to the source of a problem when technical skill alone will not.

- They are *communicative*. To create a program, software developers must understand precisely what needs to be done, and to understand this, they must be capable of acquiring substantial knowledge about the problem from those who need a solution.

- They are *consultative*. In many cases, the people who need a solution do not have a firm understanding of what needs to be solved and have little idea of how to solve it. Rather, customers have a general understanding of the objectives that must be met. Software developers must be capable of guiding their customers toward an understanding and definition of what is required to solve the problem.

- They are *disciplined*. To develop and build effective, robust software, developers must integrate hundreds, and sometimes thousands, of individual components. And they must do this in a disciplined fashion, else chaos will reign.

- They are *retrospective*. Much of what software developers do is based on work that has already been done. They must be good historians (maybe "archaeologist" is a better term)—able to understand previous work, and then extend or adapt it to accommodate present needs.

- They are *pragmatic*. Idealists rarely last in this business, for the development of computer-based systems demands pragmatic trade-offs that leave no one completely satisfied. Idealists will iterate endlessly, attempting to satisfy all of their ideals. As the project falls further behind schedule, the customer is no closer to a solution at all. Pragmatists recognize that a compromise solution will often provide significant benefit, even if it leaves a few things out.

- They are *skilled*. To develop software that satisfies customers' needs, the developer must have a firm grasp of the vast array of tools and techniques available today. The days of the coding pad and seat-of-the-pants approach to software development are behind us (fortunately).

- They are *organized*. Even with the best skills, attitudes, and technology, software developers will get into trouble unless the approach to building large-scale, industry-quality systems has been organized so that everyone working on the project can integrate the individual's work smoothly with others'.

- They are *adaptable*. There are few technologies that are changing as rapidly as software. In little more than forty years, the field has evolved from coders entering programs by manipulating toggle switches on the computer to software engineers using specialized methods and tools to create systems equal to billions of toggle switch settings. As the technology changes, software developers must change with it.

- They are *optimistic*. Without a certain degree of optimism, no one could or would work in the business of software development. Secretly, software developers expect that all of their programs will work the first time, that their customers will never need to request any changes, and that the outrageously short development schedule will somehow be met. Unrealistic? Maybe. But it is this trait that allows software developers to achieve real success.

- They have a *sense of humor*. There are many things about the business that are laughable—even if the laughter does not come from all quarters at the same time.

No one could possibly exhibit all of these personality traits (as we said, some of them are contradictory). There are few software developers who are exceptionally creative, extraordinarily well-organized, remarkably capable, and at the same time adaptable, pragmatic, and optimistic. (They also leap tall buildings in a single bound!)

In addition to these positive traits, some developers exhibit negative characteristics:

- They are *poor writers* who hate to spend time documenting. Much of software developers' time is spent trying to figure out what their predecessors have done—a difficult task because little information about the program exists. Yet the same developers who curse the lack of information about an old program will resist creating similar information about a current program, and lamentably will be cursed by their successors.

- They are often *opinionated* and sometimes *obstinate*. When discussing new technical ideas, many software developers resist anything new, calling on their many years of experience. The problem is that sometimes this experience is actually only one year of work repeated many times.

- They are *loners*. Modern software projects demand a team approach. Systems are too large and time-lines are too short for one person to do it all. Yet, some software developers have never learned to work with others.

- They are *cynics*. The school of hard knocks has taught many software developers to become unwavering disciples of Murphy's Law. Although this is often a reasonable defense against the vagaries of project work, some staffers become so cynical that they make Murphy's prediction a self-fulfilling prophecy.

In reality, most managers are willing to hire someone with one or two negative traits, as long as the same person also has three or four beneficial traits. That's why work classifications within the software world are often tuned to the traits for a particular job. For example, an analyst needs excellent interpersonal skills and must be a capable consultant and problem solver. However, an analyst need not be an expert in the latest technology nor be exceptionally creative in the design and construction of programs.

It Takes All Kinds to Build a Team

Just as no single software developer is likely to have all of the character traits just described, few individuals can be equally effective in all the roles demanded by modern software development. That's why many software projects are *team* projects.

Teams may be composed of any of a number of roles, but they must always include a pragmatist, problem owner, and problem solver. A *technical manager* may play the role of the pragmatist, organizing the project so that other skills can be applied. A *customer* suggests the problem to be solved and attempts (sometimes poorly) to define the need in an unambiguous way. An *analyst* is the problem solver, communicating and consulting with the customer, and suggesting how technology can be applied to solve the problem. The *software engineer* shares the role of problem solver, in applying the technology through a combination of creativity, technical skill, obsessiveness, and optimism to get the job done.

On really good teams, each of the players can pinch hit—that is, a software engineer can be communicative and consultative when the need arises, and a technical manager can get into the trenches and do some real work. But all teams are not equal—even when good people populate them. In their book *Peopleware,* DeMarco and Lister discuss this issue:

> We tend to use the word *team* fairly loosely in the business world, calling any group of people assigned to work together a "team." But many of these groups just don't seem like teams. They don't have a common definition of success or any identifiable team spirit. Something is missing. What is missing is a phenomenon we call *jell.*
>
> A jelled team is a group of people so strongly knit that the whole is greater than the sum of the parts. . . .

Once a team begins to jell, the probability of success goes up dramatically. The team can become almost unstoppable, a juggernaut for success. . . . They don't need to be managed in the traditional sense, and they certainly don't need to be motivated. They've got *momentum.* [*]

DeMarco and Lister contend (and we agree) that members of jelled teams are significantly more productive, happier, and more motivated than average. They share a common goal, a common culture, and in many cases, a "sense of eliteness" that makes them unique.

To illustrate effective use of a jelled team, consider the case of a start-up software company suffering from the product quality blues.

Version 1.0 of their product, which was produced in a garage, revolutionized the industry and succeeded beyond the company's wildest dreams. Orders poured in, venture capital materialized, the company grew, and customer requests led to versions 1.1, 1.2, and 2.0. Unfortunately, the blitzkrieg atmosphere that characterized its product development cycle left little time for solid software engineering practices, and the quality of the product slipped. Release 2.0.1 (intended to fix errors in version 2.0) created more problems than it solved.

"When customers began calling me to complain about bugs, I knew that we had to do something," said the twenty-eight-year-old VP of Software Engineering. "So I decided to form a software quality assurance and testing (QAT) team."

Unfortunately, not one of the company's twenty-four software developers volunteered. "Problem was, nobody wanted to join," the VP said, "and our culture here demands that people sign up for any task."

Undaunted, management hired an experienced QAT manager and offered a twenty percent sign-up bonus for any technical person who would join the team. More importantly, they char-

---

[*] T. DeMarco and T. Lister, *Peopleware* (New York: Dorset House Publishing, 1987), p. 123.

acterized the QAT team as a prestigious assignment—one for which only the very best people would be rotated. That did it. The team had more applicants than positions. But the challenge was to make the team jell.

The VP explained the company's approach: "Luckily, the QAT manager had gone through this before and worked hard to get everyone signed up to a simple goal—making every product, every release, every update coming down the line fail! The team adopted a name: *The Bug Busters* and thrived on breaking programs. Nothing gave them a bigger thrill than uncovering an error."

"We have a common goal on this team and we work collectively to come up with devilish tests that will drive the development group nuts," laughs the QAT manager.

"Have you ever seen the little decals that football players have on their helmets?" he asks. "Coaches give those out for particularly good play. I give out little bug decals when someone finds a really subtle or interesting error. QAT team members put them on the white boards in their offices. Might sound hokey, but it works."

Before long, there was a waiting list of people who wanted to join the team. Faces changed as people rotated back onto development assignments, but the effectiveness of the team continued. More importantly, the quality of the company's software products improved dramatically.

The Roles People Play

Within the software community, there is an increasing trend toward specialization. Specific individuals are assigned area expert roles— that is, an individual specializes in databases or computer graphics, telecommunications, or operating systems. Work in the area is assigned to the specialist or the specialist is used as a consultant by a development team.

In medicine, we no longer find many general practitioners. The depth of knowledge required for each area of medical specialization demands dedicated attention. On the down side, though, problems that cross areas of specialization sometimes aren't addressed very well. To solve this problem, most hospitals assign an attending physician, who (in theory at least) coordinates the specialists, ensuring that their actions don't work at cross purposes to one another and that things don't fall into the cracks.

Similarly, as the trend toward technological specialization in software continues, we may need an *attending engineer,* a software engineer with enough general knowledge to ensure that the program survives the ministrations of the software specialists. Today, this role is often played by the technical manager, who coordinates the activities of all team members as well as those outsiders who work with the team.

Technical specialization is not the only change that we see. In the early days, programmers worked on different assignments for varying periods, working on a database system one week and a quality control package the next. Today's software developers are more domain-focused, working in only one applications area—transaction processing, end-user computing, manufacturing software, and so forth.

In addition to people who build the software, there are also those who analyze the process for building the software in an effort to improve it. The *process analyst* takes measurements, solicits opinions, and generally assesses the effectiveness of the software engineering process.

A variation on this new role, sometimes called a *quality analyst* or *quality engineer,* involves a software technologist serving as the customers' in-house representative—that is, the quality analyst ensures that good software engineering practices are being followed, that standards and procedures for software development are being maintained, and that developers are working to produce a high-quality product. The quality analyst also works with software developers to isolate the causes of any defects in delivered products and eliminate them from the process.

The Sorcerer and the Apprentice

We have identified formal and quasi-formal job classifications and specializations, but there are also informal roles. Every software development organization has a resident *sorcerer*—someone with outstanding technical skills, often controversial opinions, and an attitude that does not suffer fools gladly.[*] Sorcerers make enormous contributions to a software development organization, both in a technical role and as teachers.

Sorcerers may have *apprentices,* junior staff members who work under their tutelage and who progress more rapidly than those who do not. Some of the apprentices become sorcerers themselves.

The sorcerer is a software superhero. In the tradition of Superman's Jimmy Olsen and Batman's Robin, a sorcerer has a *grunt.* Grunts are journeymen software developers who work for the sorcerers, but choose not to learn very much from them. Grunts are happy with their lot in life: implementing small parts of large systems that are conceived by the sorcerer. Grunts don't want the responsibility and don't care about the rewards associated with management, and sometimes don't have the intellectual capability or the innate desire to become a sorcerer. During the time it takes a sorcerer to learn, apply, modify, and accept or reject a new technology, the grunt is just beginning to learn what the sorcerer is ready to throw away.

Yet, grunts are real contributors. Without staff members who are willing to do drudge work—and there is plenty of drudge work

---

[*]The sorcerer is known by many names: *wizard, superstar,* and *guru* to name a few, but you'll never see these titles on a business card. However, there are more than a few software people who would gladly substitute the job title "sorcerer" for "programmer" or "engineer."

in the software development process—progress would grind to a halt.

Some grunts (and very few sorcerers) become *maintainers,* software archaeologists who study the past and adapt that knowledge to the present. They are responsible for the care and feeding of existing programs. While many regard the maintainer as a pretty mundane role, we believe it conjures up images of Indiana Jones. The maintainer is part archaeologist, part technician, and part adventurer!

Every day, the maintainer enters an ancient software jungle in which dangerous snakes lurk behind every program component, booby traps lie hidden on every control path, and the logical foliage is so thick and twisted as to be impenetrable. Using experience and a few primitive tools, the software maintainer makes the daily journey into the jungle, sometimes bitten by snakes, captured in a booby trap, or lost in a maze of twisted logic. More than a few old programs have, in fact, become the "temple of doom."

Learning the Craft

There is no single way musicians learn to play competently. Some people begin fooling around with an instrument as a hobby; others receive formal training. Some learn the underlying music theory in a classroom setting; others absorb the theory by applying their craft. Some learn to play many instruments; others know only one. Some compose music for many people to play; others can play very well, but couldn't write more than a simple tune.

Learning software is similar to learning music. Some people receive all of their training on the job, while others are trained more formally, in college. Some learn many programming languages and tools, while others live their entire technical lives speaking only C or COBOL. Some become systems architects (the sorcerers described earlier), while others are happy as grunts.

There is no formula for learning to be a software developer or engineer, but there are three general ways to receive training:

- Formal classroom training at technical schools, colleges, or universities through a variety of courses and degree programs —courses in the whole range of software development, as well as programs in computer science, computer engineering, information science, management information systems, or software engineering. In addition, other disciplines (such as business, electrical engineering, physics, and mathematics) require software knowledge, and graduates from these disciplines often migrate into software work.

- On-the-job training during apprenticeships, through in-house courses, public seminars, video-based training, and computer-assisted instruction.

- Informal training throughout a career, from reading, attending professional conferences, and talking with technical peers.

Colleges and universities play a major role in software education, and their importance is growing. In 1980, fewer than ten schools in the United States offered even a single course entitled "Software Engineering." By 1990, more than three hundred such courses were being offered throughout the U.S. and hundreds more at universities worldwide. While a good sign, these data are somewhat misleading. For one thing, the quality and relevance of education varies greatly from school to school. Most curricula do a good job of introducing basic theory: programming techniques, data structures, compiler design, and automata theory. But other software topics are often missing. For example, thirty to forty percent of all effort during a software development project is spent on testing. Yet fewer than five percent of all computer science and other software-related programs have a formal course in software testing. This means that most graduates know relatively little about an activity that may absorb forty percent of their working life.

Second, many students acquire bad habits in their academic courses, like adopting quick-and-dirty approaches to coding. These must be unlearned when they move into a more structured industry setting. Third, industry projects demand a team-oriented approach, but most students work alone throughout their academic careers and are never introduced to proper team behavior or team-building skills.

As a result, employers find they must reinforce and expand the software-related training that a new-hire has received as an undergraduate. It is estimated that U.S. industry spends almost a billion dollars on software-related training (including the cost of courses, instructors, travel, and salaries). This represents a significant expenditure, but surprisingly, it's not enough!

The vast majority of software practitioners are under-trained. Unlike other professions—law, medicine, and education—in which members may be required to attend several days of training per year to stay up to date, software-related training is viewed as a reward to be offered only when the work load is light, times are good, and projects are on schedule. The irony is that projects often fall behind schedule because technical people don't understand the software development methods that might keep them on schedule. Because the project is behind schedule, staff members don't have the time to obtain training. As they fall further behind schedule, the likelihood of training is diminished even further. A vicious cycle is created.

When we consider the rapid rate of change in computing technology and the fact that many new hires are under-trained, one or two weeks of training per year for software developers is a minimum requirement to develop and maintain proficiency. Most software people do not receive this level of continuing training, and the penalty for this situation is harsh: poor performance and unacceptable product quality.

So sorcerers, apprentices, grunts, and their managers attempt to do the next best thing: learn what they can on their own. But the roadblock this time comes from within. Our own informal survey of software practitioners indicates that fewer than twenty-five percent read any technical journal on a regular basis; fewer than ten percent have read any recently published technical book in the last year. Nearly all who don't read give the same excuse, "No time."

On a more positive note, almost all read industry trade papers or magazines occasionally. This means that most software people want to keep up with new products, the most recent salary survey, and an occasional technical article, but few dedicate themselves to self-training. They learn on the job, and in fairness, they can learn a great deal in this way alone.

Who Is the Customer?

In the software world, "customer" can refer to an individual, an organizational entity, or a market segment. Because customers wear so many different masks, software developers are intuitively wary of them. To understand the interaction between a customer and a seller, let's examine the customer in a more familiar surrounding.

Assume your ten-year-old family car is ready to die and you know it's time to buy a new car.

"I'm looking for some basic transportation," you say (less than enthusiastically) to the salesperson. As your eyes dart around the showroom floor, you describe your purchase, "What I need is good gas mileage, a lot of trunk space, four doors, and I absolutely can't spend more than $12,000."

As the customer, you may feel uncomfortable or enthusiastic, weary or exhilarated, apprehensive or calm, and confused or knowledgeable, all at the same time.

If the salesperson is ethical, he or she will show you a product that meets your stated needs: "We have just what you want. Our All Suburban Vehicle (ASV) gets thirty-two mpg, has four doors, and lots of trunk space, and lists for only $11,990. It sounds like we've got a match!"

But as the salesperson talks, your eyes continue roving the showroom. "Before we go out to the lot," you say, "I just want to take a look at the car over there."

There is a heartbeat pause, and a widening smile on the salesperson's face. "You mean the XZ-91 Sportscoupe?"

"Yeah, I'm just curious."

The XZ-91 Sportscoupe costs $23,500, gets fifteen mpg, has two doors, and a trunk that is slightly bigger than a bread box. But your pragmatism has given way to emotion. Your well-defined requirements are rapidly changing.

Which car will you buy? Some customers cannot be swayed from their original requirements. The specification (good mileage, a lot of trunk space, four doors, and costing no more than $12,000) is everything. Emotion doesn't enter into the picture. Those customers will buy the ASV.

Others are more emotional. Although they begin with one set of requirements, they are led astray by flash. Even if they feel rather strongly the original requirements are correct, they can't resist the glitz of higher performance and good looks, and they buy the XZ-91. The choice is based on the personality of the customer.

No question, there are substantial differences between buying software and buying a car. Software customers have different needs and different personalities. But in one way, all customers are alike. Whether the customer is buying a new car, a VCR, or a sophisticated software-based system, *the combination of pragmatism and emotion governs the interplay between the buyer and seller.* Software customers begin by requesting a Chevy and often leave driving a Cadillac.

To summarize, these are the characteristics of software customers:

- *Customers have different needs.* Some know what they want; others only know what they don't want. Some customers are willing to sweat the details, while others are satisfied with vague promises.

- *Customers have different personalities.* Some enjoy being customers—the tension, the negotiation, the psychological rewards of obtaining a good product at an acceptable price. Others prefer not to be customers at all. Some will happily accept almost anything that is delivered and make the best of a poor product; others will complain bitterly when quality is lacking. Some will show their appreciation when quality is good; a few will complain no matter what.

- *Customers also have varied associations with their suppliers.* Some know the product and producer well; others may be faceless, communicating with the producer only by written correspondence and a few hurried telephone calls.

- *Customers are often contradictory.* They want everything yesterday and they want it for free. Often, the producer or seller is caught among the customers' own contradictions.

Shopping for Software

We can gain additional insight into the role of the software customer by exploring the different types of products the shopper can buy:

- *Consumer products*—prepackaged PC-based software that has become commonplace for both personal and business computing. Among the thousands of software consumer products are spreadsheets, desktop publishing software, drawing packages, databases, home entertainment products, and dozens of other categories. Products in this domain typically cost between $39 and $495.

- *Business products*—prepackaged software that is used on computers of all sizes and sold by huge computer vendors (like IBM, Digital Equipment Corp., and Hewlett-Packard) and hundreds of smaller software companies. These products address business needs from the mundane (accounting) to the esoteric (piping design). Business products typically cost between a few hundred and hundreds of thousands of dollars.

- *Custom products*—software that is specifically designed and implemented to meet a customer's requirements. The cost of such products can range from tens of thousands to millions of dollars.

- *Custom systems*—software that is developed as one component of a custom computer-based system. For example, an automated teller network for a bank is composed of totally customized hardware, software, and database. An avionics system makes use of specialized hardware and custom-built software that is embedded within a plane's controls. The cost of such systems typically ranges from hundreds of thousands to tens of millions of dollars.

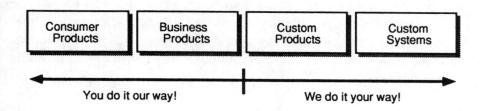

The spectrum of software product types.

In the first category, there is virtually no direct interaction between the customer and the producer. Buyers decide they need the product (a spreadsheet, for example), investigate what's available often by reading published comparisons and reviews, and buy the product of choice.

Customers who want to purchase a business product are more demanding. Requirements are often indicated in writing; benchmark tests are conducted to compare product features; the software developer is possibly asked to make "a few minor changes" to customize the package; maintenance agreements are explored; and on-site support and training are considered.

Further along the spectrum, acquisition of a custom product makes new demands on the customer because a complete set of requirements must be specified. Only then can the software developer build the custom product with some assurance that customer expectations will be met.

Too often, unfortunately, customers who decide they want custom products built are unsure of what they really need. They rely on the developer to fill in the details as the product is being built, or they write an ambiguous specification and then keep changing their requirements. Both approaches are recipes for disaster.

At the far end of the product spectrum are custom systems, which are complicated by simultaneous development of many systems components (including hardware, software, and database). Because of their complexity, these products are acquired only by experienced customers who are as knowledgeable as the developers in the technology and who can monitor every phase of the development process.

Communicating with the Customer

As the geographic and organizational distance between software developers and their customers increases, the degree of formality that governs their transactions must also increase. Communication with an office mate who is a customer is easier than communication with a colleague located in another country.

However, geographic separation is not always the determining factor that governs the quality of the communication. Two engineering groups working on software for the same custom system may be separated by hundreds or even thousands of miles. Yet, much informal communication can occur (via phone, fax, or electronic mail) because the groups are both working to a single specification, have the same manager, and have a single goal.

Conversely, an engineering group may have a marketing/sales group as a customer. Though separated by a hundred feet, the communication between these two organizational entities must be rather formal. Each has different objectives—one to sell the product and increase revenue, the other to build the product and improve quality. Although these objectives should not conflict, they cause each constituency to view the world differently.

> "Look, we've got a $1.5 million sale locked up, if you guys in engineering can make a few small changes that the customer needs," says the salesperson to the software engineering manager. The changes look simple enough and the reward for making them is obvious.
>
> But the engineering manager looks at things a bit differently. "We can't possibly make these changes and still deliver the system on November 1st," frowns the manager. "Each one of your so-called small changes has a significant impact across the entire system."
>
> "What!" wails the salesperson. "You promised November 1st and I already promised those changes."

Ideally, to avoid conflicts like this one, the company's management must establish procedures that require engineering and marketing/sales to work together. Before engineering builds a new system, marketing/sales should survey the customer base to determine what features are most likely to be changed and where customization is likely to be requested. The software engineering group then designs the product with these contingencies in mind.

In their oft-quoted *In Search of Excellence,* Thomas Peters and Robert Waterman, Jr., comment on how the best companies regard customer service:

> In observing the excellent companies, and specifically the way they interact with customers, what we found most striking was the constant presence of *obsession.* This characteristically occurred as a seemingly unjustifiable overcommitment to some form of quality, reliability, or service. Being customer-oriented doesn't mean that our excellent companies are slouches when it comes to technological or cost performance. But they do seem to us more driven by their direct orientation to their customers than by technology or by a desire to be the low-cost producer.[*]

Both software developers and their customers would do well to heed this message. Developers must be obsessed with quality, reliability and service, the underlying goals of good software engineering. They must clearly understand who their customers really are and what the product requirements are. Only then can they judge quality. If a custom product or system is to be built, they should not exclude customers from early design decisions, because exclusion will result in misunderstanding and missed expectations.

Customers, too, must be obsessed with developing a clear statement of what is required. They should not delegate this work, because doing so will relinquish their control over the end product. They should not avoid indicating areas where uncertainty exists, because doing this will mislead the developers and result in antagonism later in the project.

---

[*]T.J. Peters and R.H. Waterman, Jr., *In Search of Excellence: Lessons from America's Best-Run Companies* (New York: Harper & Row, 1982), p. 157.

To quote Glen Myers, a writer on software engineering topics:

> We try to solve the problem by rushing through the design process so that enough time is left at the end of the project to uncover the errors that were made because we rushed through the design process.[*]

In many human endeavors, obsession is a dangerous trait. For the customer who must acquire software and the engineers who must build it, obsession is a virtue.

The User

> While dressing for work one morning, a businessman noticed his best suit was becoming threadbare. "I'll stop in the garment district on the way into work," he said, "and buy myself another suit." The businessman knew that good suits could be acquired there at low cost.
>
> In the garment district, he saw a shop with the sign "I.M. Genius—Expert Tailor" over the door. Figuring that anybody with a name like that surely must be an expert, the businessman went in. The tailor took his measurements and told the businessman to return the next day to pick up his suit. Thrilled that a suit could be made so quickly, the businessman left with a smile on his face.
>
> The next day, the businessman returned to the tailor shop and tried on the new suit. To his horror, one arm was longer than the other, the buttons didn't match, it was too tight in the shoulders, and the knees were baggy. "Look at this suit!" he screamed at the tailor, "You've done a terrible job."
>
> "No problem," said the tailor, "just hunch your shoulders, bend your arm, lean forward a bit, bend your knees, and the suit will look fine." The businessman did as instructed, and the suit did seem to fit better. He left the shop feeling duped.
>
> As he walked down the street, a passerby stopped to compliment him on his suit.

---

[*] G.J. Myers, *Composite/Structured Design* (New York: Van Nostrand Reinhold Co., 1978), p. 2.

"What tailor did you use?" asked the passerby.

The businessman, feeling better about his new suit, gave the man directions to the tailor's shop.

But as the man turned to go, the businessman couldn't help asking, "Why is it that you want to go to my tailor?"

"That's obvious," said the passerby, "he must be a genius to be able to fit a cripple like you!"

This familiar parable of the Genius Tailor has much to tell us about users of computer software. For the first thirty years of the computing era, users were forced to "contort" their natural mode of interaction and communication to accommodate the computer. They had to "talk" to the computer by typing—an unnatural (and sometimes painful) activity for many people—and had to use a formal, unforgiving syntax. Leave out a space or forget a comma? The computer (actually the software) wouldn't accept it. Worse, the system might accept it, but do the wrong thing.

In his book on user interface design, Ben Shneiderman summarizes the current situation nicely:

> Frustration and anxiety are a part of daily life for many users of computerized information systems. They struggle to learn command language or menu selection systems that are supposed to help them do their job. Some people encounter such serious cases of computer shock, terminal terror, or network neurosis that they avoid using computerized systems. These electronic-age maladies are growing more common, but help is on the way. *

It has taken a long time for the countless user complaints to filter back to software developers. In the early days, the technology was so new and the capabilities so impressive, that a few small difficulties in interaction were the price one had to pay. But as time passed,

---

*B. Shneiderman, *Designing the User Interface: Strategies for Effective Human-Computer Interaction* (Reading, Mass.: Addison-Wesley, 1987), p. *v*.

users began to demand ease of use in addition to quality and quantity of output.

"I'm sick and tired of trying to figure out why the data I enter into the mainframe system aren't being accepted," says a frazzled user at a large insurance company. "The system keeps saying 'miscellaneous data error' and I have no idea what it means. My PC programs never do this to me. They're easy to understand and easy to use. They're user friendly, and that's what our information systems people still haven't learned to build."

PC software has, in fact, changed the expectations of a generation of computer users. Users now expect "friendliness," and resist any program that doesn't have it. Today, an unfriendly PC program will not survive in the marketplace. But the human friendliness of software for larger computers varies dramatically, and the users who work with these programs are losing patience.

Who are the users? Today, just about everyone. At one end of the spectrum, users have no educational prerequisite, no computer training, and little if any understanding of the internal workings of the program they are using. A personal computer buyer, a customer using an ATM at the local bank, the cashier at a grocery store, a telephone caller using a voice mail system, a homeowner who is programming a new VCR—there are very few people in an industrialized country who are not software users.

At the other end of the spectrum, there are users who must have a specific educational background, who receive specialized training, and who do understand the function of the program being applied. An engineer who is using a computer-aided design system, a scientist monitoring a computer-controlled experiment, a manager planning a project using a scheduling tool, an accountant entering data for preparing a client's income taxes—all are professionals who use a program that has been specifically designed to assist in their work.

Finally, there are many users who sit somewhere between the ends of the user spectrum. These users have an acceptable educational background, but no specific training in the use of computers and software. They have a general idea of how the computer works, but no detailed knowledge of the workings of a program. They represent the majority of active computer users.

The People—Final Comments

Software people are no different from any other group of humans. There are leaders and there are followers. There are skilled practitioners and there are incompetents. There are outgoing optimists who make significant contributions and introspective cynics who make significant contributions. There are sorcerers, whose skill is the stuff of legends, and grunts who are the foot soldiers in the march toward high-technology systems. There are those who are formally trained in software engineering, and others who simply drift into the business. There are customers who know precisely what they want and others who change their mind every six hours. And then there are the users, who must make the best of the efforts of everyone else. All of them have one thing in common—they are connected by a software thread.

The Daydream

The Workshop

8

What They Do
and How They Do It

Because if Quality exists in the object, then you must explain just why scientific instruments are unable to detect it. . . . On the other hand, if Quality is subjective, existing only in [the eye of] the observer, then this Quality that you make so much of is just a fancy name for whatever you like. ... Quality is not objective ... It doesn't reside in the material world. ... Quality is not subjective ... It doesn't reside merely in the mind. *

---

* R. Pirsig, *Zen and the Art of Motorcycle Maintenance: An Inquiry into Values* (New York: William Morrow & Co., 1974), pp. 228-29, 237.

Quality is a challenging concept. When we think about a high-quality automobile or fine wine, we combine objective assessment of the attributes of the object with subjective evaluation of its "goodness." This is particularly difficult to do with software. The software object cannot be observed in the same way as a physical entity. Quality can be assessed, but sight, sound, smell, and touch don't help very much.

What is high-quality computer software and how is it built? What do software developers do when faced with a new problem and how do they solve it? These are the questions we'll address in this chapter.

Software Quality

In his landmark book *Quality Is Free,* Philip Crosby suggests an amusing analogy between quality and sex:

- Everyone is for it. (Under certain conditions, of course).
- Everyone feels they understand it. (Even though they wouldn't want to explain it.)
- Everyone thinks execution is merely a matter of following natural inclinations. (After all, we do get along somehow.)
- And, of course, most people feel that all problems in these areas are caused by other people. (If only *they* would take time to do things right.)*

Crosby's discussion of quality does not refer explicitly to software, yet it is applicable to software in every respect. Let's examine his statements in the context of real-life situations.

Everyone is for software quality, under certain conditions.

A few years ago, I (RSP) was working with a large computer vendor that had recently delivered an operating system rife with er-

---

* P. Crosby, *Quality Is Free* (New York: McGraw-Hill, 1979), pp. 13-14.

rors. Customers became gravely concerned, and the software people screamed: "Management forced us to meet the delivery date even after we told them the programs weren't ready." Managers blamed market pressures: "Certain levels of revenue had to be achieved and this new operating systems product was the only way to do it."

Here's a snippet from the conversation with the company's Vice President of Engineering:

RSP: Your technical people are telling me they were forced to deliver software before it was ready.

VP: That's probably true, but it doesn't tell the whole story.

RSP: What do you mean?

VP: What the technical people don't realize is we were strapped for revenue during this quarter and we desperately needed the dollars that could be generated through the release of this systems software. If we didn't get the revenue, we'd have to cut expenses in some other way.

RSP: But aren't you worried about your customers' reaction to shoddy software?

VP: Sure we are, but we were between a rock and a hard place. Without the revenue, we would have had to lay off two hundred people. Given a choice between releasing a product before it was quite ready and being laid off, which do you think my technical people would have chosen?

No one wants to release a product before it is ready. Everyone is for quality, but when push comes to shove, decisions that lead to low quality are sometimes made. In the situation described above, the decision to ship was understandable, but not correct. In fact, this company may have lost more revenue in the long run due to ill will from its current customers, as well as lost sales once the word got around. Short-term thinking and a focus on short-term results (to the exclusion of all else) invariably leads to trouble.

We think we understand software quality, but we wouldn't want to explain it.

> We were sitting in on a meeting between the software engineering manager and the director of marketing for a large company that builds sophisticated medical instrumentation. The following conversation ensued:
>
> **Marketing director:** You guys in engineering have got to do a better job of providing us with better software. The last release of the product just doesn't cut it.
> **Engineering manager:** What do you mean? We wrote the specification, you approved it, and we built the software to spec.
> **Marketing director:** That may be, but the software just doesn't have quality.
> **Engineering manager:** OK, what do you mean by quality?
> **Marketing manager:** Well . . . dammit, the software just didn't do what we expected it to do!

From the marketers' point of view, the perception of quality may be subjective. From the software developers' point of view, quality takes on tangible attributes that have a strong bearing on fitness for use. Hewlett-Packard describes these with the acronym FURPS— functionality, usability, reliability, performance, and supportability.[*] Each of these general characteristics is further refined for software:

- *functionality* can be measured by considering the feature set and capabilities of the program, its generality and its security;
- *usability* is assessed by considering human factors, aesthetics, consistency, and documentation;

---

[*] R. Grady and D. Caswell, *Software Metrics: Establishing a Company-wide Program* (Englewood Cliffs, N.J.: Prentice-Hall, 1987), p. 159.

- *reliability* relates to the frequency and severity of errors, the ability to recover from errors, the program's accuracy, and the overall mean-time-between-failures;
- *performance* is measured by program speed, efficiency, and resource consumption, overall throughput, and response time;
- *supportability* combines the ability to test, install, configure, extend, adapt, and service a program—it is a measure of the program's maintainability.

Not every attribute is applicable in every situation. However, high-quality software exhibits high grades in the majority of attributes noted.

Everyone thinks execution is merely a matter of following natural inclinations.

In an effort to improve the quality of the software they build, a large telecommunications company spent much time, money, and effort writing a detailed standards and procedures document for software development. After nearly a year's worth of effort, the document was released along with appropriate management memos encouraging all software developers to use it.

About a year later, I (RSP) conducted a software engineering assessment for this organization. One morning, I sat in on a management presentation that among other things described the software engineering standards and procedures document in some detail. The presenter indicated that the document was the backbone of software quality within the organization and was used by most, if not all, the software developers.

That afternoon, while wandering around the development area, I stopped to chat with a software developer. As she explained the design work being done, I asked whether the model's format and content corresponded to the one outlined in the standards and procedures document. She paused for just a moment and said, "Well, sure, I use a set of standards for developing my designs."

"No," I responded, "what I mean is the company's standards and procedures document."

Again, she paused, stood up, and looked over into the cubicle next door. "Sal," she asked, "do you know anything about a standards and procedures document?"

I was sitting down and when no sound came from the next cubicle, I craned my neck to see what was going on. The young man in the next cubicle had leaned over the divider to the adjacent work space and was talking to the person next door. That person then stood up, and in classic domino fashion, asked the person in the cubicle next to his. This went on until it reached the group's unit manager.

At this point, the manager stood up, looked across the work area, and asked, "Who is this guy and why is he asking these questions?"

For this company, the natural inclination was to develop a comprehensive standards and procedures document, dictate its use, and expect that only good things would follow. The reality was considerably different. Of the people who were given the manual, few used it on a regular basis and a fair number admitted that they never even opened it. New hires didn't even know it existed.

Quality problems are always someone else's fault.

A large systems house won the bid to build the computer-based control system for a city's mass transit line. After extensive software engineering, the system was implemented and underwent thorough testing. For the grand opening, all the local dignitaries, including the Mayor, as well as the Governor and the chief executive officers of all the major contractors that worked on the transit system planned to attend the ribbon cutting ceremony. The print, broadcast, and cable news media were expected to cover the event.

On the day before the ceremony, an error was discovered in the collision control system that would not guarantee separation between trains. At first, the problem was attributed to faulty hardware. The offending hardware devices were replaced, but the problem remained. Next, the software became suspect, but extensive tests indicated the algorithm was solid.

Finger pointing began, with the hardware and the software people blaming each other. With twelve hours to show time, the CEO of the prime contractor learned of the problem and the bickering between the hardware and software engineering organizations. He reacted in his typical take-no-prisoners style.

"You tell all of them," he hissed, "that if they don't work together to solve this thing, I'm going to put the software people in one train, the hardware people in another train, point the trains at one another, and let 'em rip. If as they claim there's nothing wrong with the hardware and software, they don't have a thing to worry about."

With four hours to go, the problem was fixed. [*]

What They Did

At one time or another, we all lament the passing of the good old days. We miss the simplicity, the personal touch, the emphasis on quality that we remember as the trademarks of the time. Carpenters reminisce about the days when houses were built with mahogany and oak, and beams were set without nails. Engineers talk about an earlier era when one person did all the design (and did it right) and then built the thing on the shop floor. In those days, people did good work and stood behind it.

How far back must we travel to reach the good old days? Both carpentry and engineering have a history that is well over two thousand years old. The disciplined approach to work, the standards

---

[*]For those inquiring minds who must know the culprit, a subtle timing error in the computer software was to blame.

that guide each task, and the step-by-step approach have all evolved through centuries of experience. Software engineering has a much shorter history, measured only in terms of decades. Yet, programmers who remember like to recount the good old days.

The earliest programmers were often the same people who built the computers, for programming (or coding) could be performed only by those who understood the machine's inner workings. During the 1950s, that was very few people indeed. Just as the craftsmen of old understood every nuance of their materials and tools, these programmers played the commands to the computer (its *instruction set*) like a fine instrument. This arcane and mysterious instruction set bore little resemblance to modern programming languages.

A programmer from this era describes his world: "Every time I wanted to code a new instruction, I had to walk to the front of our work area. There, on the wall was a large blackboard painted with a large checkerboard. Each square of the checkerboard represented a memory location in the machine, and we all had to sign out every memory location that we needed before we used it!"

In this milieu, programming was born.

The first programs, although primitive by today's standards, were a marvel for their time and indicated the potential that computers and software offered. As the demand grew and the machines evolved, so also did the languages that people used to communicate with the machines. Programming languages entered via punched cards, paper tape, or teletype replaced machine code as the primary mode of program description. During the 1950s, an instruction from a programmer commanded the computer to perform one micro-operation.

By the early 1960s, a statement written in FORTRAN or COBOL (the dominant programming languages of the era) could generate dozens or even hundreds of micro-operations. Newer programming languages—Algol, PL/I, Lisp, and others—enable programmers to build higher-quality programs.

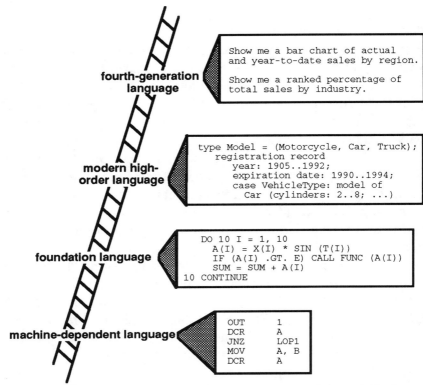

fourth-generation language

```
Show me a bar chart of actual
and year-to-date sales by region.

Show me a ranked percentage of
total sales by industry.
```

modern high-order language

```
type Model = (Motorcycle, Car, Truck);
  registration record
    year: 1905..1992;
    expiration date: 1990..1994;
  case VehicleType: model of
    Car (cylinders: 2..8; ...)
```

foundation language

```
   DO 10 I = 1, 10
     A(I) = X(I) * SIN (T(I))
     IF (A(I) .GT. E) CALL FUNC (A(I))
     SUM = SUM + A(I)
10 CONTINUE
```

machine-dependent language

```
OUT    1
DCR    A
JNZ    LOP1
MOV    A, B
DCR    A
```

Programming languages have evolved toward increasingly higher levels of abstraction. The simple program shown above for a fourth-generation language would require thousands of machine-dependent language statements to accomplish the same thing.

Although new programming languages were introduced, new tools developed, and new challenges undertaken, the basic approach to programming remained unchanged. Let's investigate why.

Throughout the 1960s and most of the 1970s, programmers were generally considered the techies in the back room, who were left alone to do whatever it was they did. But what did they do?

They were part of a freewheeling culture that exists in many companies today, a culture that believes

- Programming is problem solving.
- Problem solving at its best is creative.
- Creativity, in its purist form, should be free of any constraints.
- Therefore, programming should be free of any constraints.

Using this logical progression as a mantra, proponents of the culture resisted any attempt to impress discipline on the software development process. Their basic approach to programming can be summarized as follows:

1. Someone identified a problem for the computer to solve.
2. Coding began immediately. After a few preliminary discussions with the problem-initiator to describe the problem, a programmer began writing code to implement a solution. (Sometimes, iteration occurred. Realizing that they really didn't understand the problem, programmers would try to gain a better understanding and might even show the person who needed the solution a sample of what the program already could do.)
3. The program was debugged. The preliminary version of the program was tested to determine if it worked as desired and after problems were uncovered, changes were made to the program to make it work. The program then would be retested.
4. The program was put into service. A user other than the programmer was allowed to use the program.
5. Modifications were requested. Within a period of days or weeks, the user verified what the program could do, but also what it couldn't do. A list of changes went to the programmer.
6. The programmer modified the original program as requested, but often, the modifications generated side effects that required still additional corrections and more changes.
7. The process continued from step 4.

This seven-step approach to programming established the foundation for a culture that still exists today.

From 1970 to 1980, dramatic changes occurred in computing technology, accompanied by equally significant changes in software applications. Computer graphics, real-time systems, database management, networks, telecommunications, embedded systems, artificial intelligence, and a variety of other software-oriented technologies were introduced during this time. The size of programming projects grew from a few people to dozens and sometimes hundreds of programmers. The complexity of applications grew by orders of magnitude: from a single program that generates paychecks to banking networks that serve hundreds of thousands of users worldwide and that comprises millions of lines of code.

This rapid pace of technological change during the 1970s and early 1980s demanded more and better software. Yet, the prevailing culture for building computer programs could not respond rapidly enough. When attempts were made to change the culture, stress and disorientation resulted. Computer users and the computer industry itself began suffering from software shock.

Everyone lamented the problems associated with software, a few individuals and companies began to do something about them, and slowly the entrenched programming culture began to change. An idea that had been proposed fifteen years earlier was reintroduced to the software community. The idea was called *software engineering*.

What They Do

Software engineering remolded the freewheeling culture of programming to establish a set of beneficial limits. These limits demand that software problem solving follow a predictable sequence of events:

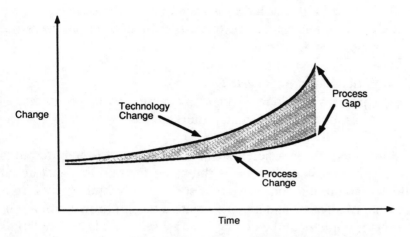

Technology change can often outpace process change.

1. The software developer and the customer carefully specify all functional and performance requirements at the beginning of a project. If these are unclear, a model of the solution (called a *prototype*) may be built to help the customer better understand what is needed. Often graphic in form, this model enables the customer to grasp the overall context more quickly, while at the same time it represents the problem in a way that can be mapped into a design.
2. The problem is analyzed so that all facets are understood.
3. The problem requirements are modeled in a way that establishes a foundation for future work; the model is reviewed to ensure that it correctly interprets the customer's desires.
4. A solution is designed using the analysis model as a basis; the design is reviewed for its quality.
5. The design is implemented in a programming language.
6. A series of test cases are designed to detect errors in the solution.

7. The implemented solution is tested and defects are corrected. Other tests are conducted to ensure the corrections have not propagated side effects.
8. The program is put into service.
9. Modifications are requested.
10. The process continues from step 1 with a focus on modifications as opposed to original requirements.

You don't have to be a scientist or an engineer to recognize this approach to building software is the same for building just about anything. To build a house, we first specify our requirements (four bedrooms, two baths, and so on); create a design (a two-story contemporary); implement the design (using a set of tools and materials standardized across the industry); inspect the house (to ensure the structure is safe for occupancy); and finally, move in. Predictably, once we move in and start using the house, we want a few things changed.

If we go through this sequence of steps for building a house, it's only logical to apply a similar sequence for a computer-based system that is considerably more complex, significantly more expensive, and often profoundly more important to a larger population of people.

Let's take our analogy between building houses and software a step further to see what the software industry can learn from the differences: [*]

• Houses are built from standard components and must meet well-defined building codes. The software industry uses few standard components and has only recently moved to establish software standards.

---

[*]Adapted from comments provided by Gene Forte, CASE Consulting Group, in a private communication.

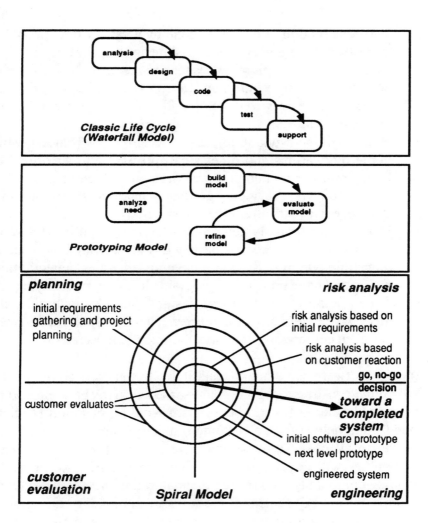

As software engineering technology has matured, different models of the software engineering process have evolved. The simple waterfall and prototyping models have given way to the spiral model, which incorporates characteristics of both while recognizing the dynamic nature of software development.

- The construction of houses is done by a variety of experts: architects, civil engineers, industrial designers, contractors, electricians, framers, plumbers, sheet rockers, painters, roofers, and so on. Until recently, one person was expected to have all the skills necessary to develop and build even large software-based systems.
- House builders work almost exclusively on new projects, while home renovations and other small projects are performed by home improvement contractors. Software developers are often responsible for every change that is made to a program or a system, even years after it has been built.
- House buyers usually determine what they want in a house by looking at existing homes, or they buy an existing house and fit their life-style to it. Software buyers sometimes demand innovation and have no existing programs to use as a prototype.
- The building industry, house designs, building materials, and tools have evolved over centuries. The time span for software has been compressed dramatically, into mere decades.

Would software developers benefit from standard components? Would the construction of computer-based systems be improved by a team of trained software specialists? Would it be helpful to have models that help software customers specify what they need? The answer to all of these questions is yes. Over time, the software community will develop the same level of maturity as the house building community, and indeed the maturation process has already begun. A growing segment of the software community is migrating from the ad hoc programming culture of the 1960s to applying the more disciplined ten-step engineering approach described earlier.

However, questions remain. Does this more disciplined approach improve the quality of the systems being built? Or does it constrain people's creativity to the detriment of the software being produced? Does it reduce the costs of development? Early evidence seems to indicate that quality is indeed improved, creativity is not dampened, and costs remain about the same or go down. Modern procedures for software development, in sum, are reducing the virulence of the software affliction and over time may ultimately lead to a cure.

How They Do It

Imagine designing and building a factory with hundreds of complex machines that produce thousands of parts to build a myriad of different products. Each machine performs a specific function. Some require raw materials to do their work, while others need parts that are produced by machine. Each machine has its own idiosyncrasies and must be carefully controlled to work with its counterparts. To complicate matters further, you know only three things at the start: the raw materials coming in, the product to be built and shipped, and the overall size limitations of the factory. You must begin the assignment without knowing specifically what each machine does, and during the project, the description of the end products changes. Sound like a daunting challenge? There's more! You're under enormous time pressure. And no one has ever built a factory quite like this before.

This nightmare illustrates the kind of challenges faced by software developers, except their factory is a computer-based system. The machines they must build and use are program components (often called *subroutines, procedures,* or more generally *modules)*. The raw materials used by some of the machines and the parts produced by all of them are information. The coordination that makes the computer run is a set of control functions that forms the skeleton of the computer program.

Let's return to the original challenge of building the factory described above. Does it make sense to begin by trying to build one of the hundreds of complex machines? Should you sort nuts and bolts for the machine, construct each of its component parts, lay out wiring, and buy vendor-supplied components as a first step? The answer is an emphatic no!

Before you can worry about the design and creation of a single machine, you first must understand the overall function and flow of the entire factory. You should know how the machines interact with each other and define how things will be coordinated. You must understand what goes into each machine and what comes out. You should describe the end product as precisely as possible, and the raw materials that enter the factory. Then, only after understanding the big picture can you focus on the machines themselves. This is simply common sense. Constructing any complex system like a factory, you begin with the big picture and proceed through a series of iterations toward the details.

But some software builders, still deeply entrenched in the culture of the 1960s, begin by focusing all of their attention and energies on a single "machine." That is, rather than expending the effort to understand the specific requirements of a problem and laying out a complete design for the entire system, these builders feel more comfortable by first coding a program component. They may do a good job of building each component, but problems often surface when the components are combined to form a system, when the system is tested, and when changes to the system are required. No one spent any time considering the big picture and how things would all fit together.

Concentrating on the big picture first is known in software engineering as a top-down approach. That is, before worrying about all the components, a software engineer should understand overall requirements and establish an architecture for the system. The role of each component is then defined in terms of both the requirements and the architecture. This approach represents good software engineering practice, supported by centuries of practical application in other disciplines, and more importantly, good common sense. As more and more organizations adopt this top-down approach, we are seeing the benefits in the form of higher-quality products that provide greater functionality.

The Iceberg

Everything that is built must be maintained. You change the oil in the car, paint the rooms in your house, or get your tennis racket re-strung. You do these things to avoid failure and the resulting ex-pense, like changing the oil to avoid replacing the engine at a much higher cost later. Or you do it because something else in the envi-ronment has changed; for example, the room is painted because a new carpet was installed. Or you change something that is operating well to enhance its function or performance, like restringing a tennis racket to improve its playing characteristics.

Unfortunately, software maintenance doesn't conform to these everyday rules, and the phrase connotes far more than simple repair and replacement. In fact, much of what is called software mainte-nance actually amounts to significant product adaptation or en-hancement. Software maintenance often changes the *design* of the product, and this is done without any blueprints to work from. That's what makes the job so difficult.

A maintenance programmer once joked, "If I treated mainte-nance of my Volkswagen the same way we treat the maintenance of software, I'd change the oil, but I'd also modify the engine to pro-duce three hundred horsepower, redesign the interior to seat nine people, and adapt the body to float on a lake!"

Software, unlike hardware, does not wear out, but it does *dete-riorate*. How can this be? When hardware is first introduced to the market, it has a high failure rate (errors per unit time) until the manu-facturing defects are corrected. The failure rate then drops to a very low level, where it remains until (often, years later) components begin wearing out. The failure rate curve then begins to creep up-ward. This graph, called the bathtub curve by hardware engineers, is true of every product, whether it's an automobile, a microwave oven, or a computer.

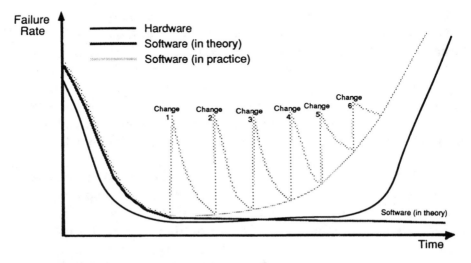

Bathtub curves for hardware and software.

If a software failure rate curve is superimposed on the bathtub curve, there is a significant difference. Like hardware, a new software product has a high failure rate until the problems are resolved and the failures drop to a very low level. Theoretically, the curve should remain low indefinitely—software doesn't wear out.

But at some point, the software undergoes change (to correct an error, to adapt it, or to enhance it), and the curve spikes. In making the change, software maintainers inadvertently introduce side effects that cause the error rate to rise. Although there are many complex reasons for software side effects, most are attributable to one cause: When software fails, the design must be modified—there are no software spare parts.

Maintainers focus on eliminating these side effects, but before getting back to the original low failure level, another change is requested, and another, and another, introducing more and more unwanted side effects. Over time, the software deteriorates.

During the early days of computing, software maintenance didn't present much of a problem. For most companies, the number of programs in use was relatively small, and their application was not critical. Errors were uncovered, functional or performance improvements were requested, and adaptations were demanded, but most of this work was accomplished with an informal phone call and a relatively quick response.

As the number and sophistication of programs and users increased, some software development organizations found that they were spending nearly as much time maintaining existing programs as they were developing new ones. Software maintenance had become an "iceberg," with most of its dangers lying invisible below the surface.

A Software Legacy

As consumers, we shy away from products with a reputation for shoddy construction. We know that keeping them working is an unacceptable burden—regardless of the price of that product. It may only take days or weeks to build a shoddy product, but the legacy of maintenance left by that product can go on for many years.

The software industry has created its own legacy. Programs developed using the undisciplined approaches of the past now are maintenance icebergs. Worse, as software maintainers struggle against time to make the corrections, enhancements, and adaptations demanded by a growing audience of users, they themselves add to the problems created by their predecessors. In the rush to get a patchwork of changes made, they take short cuts, and compound the deterioration. The iceberg looms and there appears no easy way around it.

What Should Have Been Done?

When a company builds a shoddy product, it does have options: It can stonewall, using a patchwork of maintenance and excuses to keep the thing working; or it can admit its mistake publicly, take full responsibility, and move quickly to replace the shoddy product with a better one; or it can admit its mistake privately, moving with somewhat less speed to phase out the current product and replace it with a better one.

Unfortunately, many companies that build software have opted for the first option. Rather than rebuilding unmaintainable computer programs, they chose to support a long line of patches and reactive fixes to keep the program running, keep the users quiet, and minimize short-term expenses. In reality, the changes made to keep the shoddy program running often introduced more errors than they fixed, rarely implemented the required functions in an efficient and acceptable manner, and therefore rarely satisfied end users. More changes were required, increasing expenses dramatically, and thereby angering everyone the company was trying to placate. Option one didn't work. But throughout the industry, it was attempted year after year.

When a product is unmaintainable, it should be replaced—not patched. Sadly, most companies refuse to face reality, refuse to select those critical programs that must be re-engineered rather than continually supported through a patchwork of fixes, small changes, and excuses.

The irony is that re-engineering can be easily justified in economic terms. Say it takes one or two years to develop an important software application, that application may be in service for more than two decades. The dollars spent on maintaining the program over its entire life can be from two to ten times as much as those required to develop it.

What we are talking about is a pay-now-or-pay-much-more-later situation. Unfortunately, many companies opt to pay on the installment plan, accepting continuing (and often escalating) maintenance costs over a long period of time.

Engineering Tools and Automation—A Retrospective

In the movie *Back to the Future,* the hero, Marty McFly, travels back to 1955 in a souped-up DeLorean time machine and ends up changing his future. Our journey is more mundane: to understand how engineering automation has evolved over the past forty years.

> The year is 1955. A group of mechanical and electrical engineers work with their tools: books and tables containing the formulas and algorithms needed for analysis of a problem; slide rules and mechanical calculators for ensuring the product will work; pens and pencils, drafting boards, rulers, and other paraphernalia for creating models of the product to be built. Good work was done, but it was done by hand.
>
> A decade passes and the same engineers experiment with computer-based engineering. Although some resist ("I just don't trust the results," they complain), many others embrace the new technology. The engineering process is changing.
>
> Jump to 1975. The formulas and algorithms the engineers need are now embedded in a large set of computer programs used to analyze a wide array of engineering problems. People trust the results of these programs. In fact, much of their work could not be accomplished without them. Computer graphics workstations in some companies have replaced drafting boards and related tools for creating engineering models. A link between the engineering and manufacturing work is under development, the first between computer-aided design (CAD) and computer-aided manufacturing (CAM).

Good engineering work continues, but it now depends on software. Computing and engineering have been joined inextricably.

Today, computer-aided engineering (CAE), computer-aided design, and computer-integrated manufacturing (CIM) are common in most companies. Engineering automation has not only arrived, it is an integral part of the process.

To understand the impact of automated tools on the engineering process, consider the Gillette Company and its introduction of the Sensor® razor in 1990. The Sensor represented Gillette's first new razor line in more than ten years. Peter Valorz, an engineering manager who was responsible for coordinating a design and development cycle that was compressed into eighteen months, remarked, "No one would think of doing engineering in this company without CAD, any more than you'd bring in a secretary without a word processor. . . . Not everyone was up to speed at first and some engineers resisted CAD, but once they got moving, it was like a freight train."*

Unlike Marty McFly, mechanical and electrical engineers can't go back and change the future, but software engineers can. By studying the evolution of CAE, CAD, and CIM, they can apply the lessons to the tools they build for themselves. These tools—called computer-aided software engineering or CASE—can be designed so they combine the strengths of CAE, CAD, and CIM.

People and Tools

In 1834, Scottish essayist and historian Thomas Carlyle said, "Man is a tool-using animal. . . . Without tools he is nothing, with tools he is all." Carlyle was correct, but we not only use tools, we invent

---

*"Systems Give Gillette the Razor's Edge," *Computerworld*, November 27, 1989, p. 1.

them, we adapt them, we collect them, we even grow fond of them. To the craftsman, tools are a means to extend ability, to make the job easier, to conquer the problem at hand.

The tools in a toolbox are a reflection of the skill of the craftsman. But it is not the number or variety of tools that matters. Rather, what matters is the types of tools, their diversity, and their suitability for the craft.

There's an old saying, "When the only tool you have is a hammer, every problem looks like a nail." For almost thirty years, the software developer's tool box contained only hammers for coding, and to some extent this has limited the product that software developers can build. Paraphrasing the aphorism above, When the only tool you have manipulates code, every problem looks like a solution for C or FORTRAN or COBOL or Ada or Pascal programs. And that's part of the problem!

Software developers have had no tools to help them analyze a problem, few tools to help design a solution, and only rudimentary tools to help verify functions and uncover defects. Consequently, they analyzed the problem by coding, designed the solution by coding, and tested the result by coding. The result was similar to hammering a screw into the wall.

Tools of the Trade

The best workshops have three primary components: a collection of useful tools for every step of building a product; an organized layout for finding tools quickly and efficiently; and a skilled craftsman for using the tools effectively. Software engineers now recognize that their workshops need more and varied tools beyond the CASE tools they have available today. Although CASE tools automate manual activities and improve engineering insight, they address only part of the task. One need is an organized and efficient workshop.

Today, CASE is where CAD, CAE, and CIM were in 1975: Individual CASE tools are spreading rapidly in the industry, and serious effort is underway to integrate the individual tools to form a consistent environment.

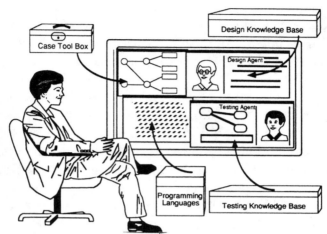

In the future, software engineers hope to have intelligent assistants to combine with existing tools.

If early experience is our guide, those companies that adopt the technology early, tune it to their specific needs, and transform their engineering culture to adapt to automation will ultimately become industry leaders and produce higher-quality products as a result. Those companies that take a wait-and-see attitude will fall behind their competition and have to scramble to catch up.

There is little doubt that CASE will affect software engineering in substantially the same way as CAE, CAD, and CIM affected their respective disciplines. However, unlike CAD/CAE/CIM, CASE is being implemented into an engineering culture that is new to many companies. The difference in impact and in acceptance is profound.

During the 1990s, the CASE tool set will grow. Second-generation CASE tools will replace their predecessors and new tools (some making use of artificial intelligence techniques) may do more than just serve the software engineer—they may take on the role of the engineer's intelligent assistant.

No one has a crystal ball. The trends associated with any new technology are often less obvious than even the experts believe, and it is difficult to be certain what CASE will be like in 1995, much less how software development will be conducted in the twenty-first century. As history indicates, change in the process through which software is developed occurs at a frustratingly slow rate.

However, there is little debate about one trend: CASE will play a role in any changes that do occur. This means that every software builder should spend the time now to evaluate this technology.

Challenges and Chain Saws

There once was a man who owned a large house. Next to the house an enormous oak tree had grown. Three feet in diameter at its base, the tree provided shade for the house and beauty to the eye.

During the winter, a storm ravaged the area. The tree survived hurricane force winds, but it tilted toward the house at an ominous angle.

"The tree must come down," said the man regretfully. "If I let it stand, it will surely fall on my house someday."

He checked with tree professionals and was shocked at the estimated cost. "I'll cut it down myself," said the man. "It will be a good challenge for my skills and I'll save money as well."

The man had cut down a few small trees on his property with a hand saw and a small ax, and he figured the job would scale upward nicely. He knew nothing about the safety procedures for cutting down large trees and less about the technical methods. He did know, however, a power tool was necessary and proceeded to the local hardware store where he bought the largest chain saw in stock.

Arriving home, he pulled the starter cord, and the chain saw roared to life. He began to cut.

At this point, one of three things happens:

1. The man cuts down the tree. It falls into his side yard. He chops it up and carts it away. Success!
2. The man cuts down the tree. It falls on his house. He hires professionals to cart it away, and hires carpenters to repair his damaged house. Failure.
3. The man cuts down the tree. It falls on him. His wife collects life insurance, pays to remove the tree and man, and lives happily ever after on the money. Finale.

The story of the man and the house can be translated to the story of the software developer and the CASE tool. Software engineering is a discipline that combines procedures, methods, and tools. All must be understood before any one is used. Too often, software engineers become enamored of the latest technology and leap to acquire the flashiest CASE tool on the market, but they fail to learn the procedures that will enable it to be applied effectively. The result is often similar to that of the homeowner's with a chain saw. With good preparation, adequate training, and careful management, CASE can help software professionals meet the challenge in the 1990s.

What Have They Learned?

In the forty years since software became a driving force behind modern technologies, organizations have learned that quality is the key to success in software development, and that to achieve software quality, new software engineering approaches are required. Poor quality leaves a nasty legacy—difficult, time-consuming, expensive, and frustrating maintenance that can haunt a software organization and its users for decades.

The industry has learned how to do it right. What software people do when they do it right is build high-quality computer programs. How they do it is through a combination of methods, procedures, and tools called software engineering.

Part IV
Making Software
Work for You

There once was a family that needed a new house. After some discussion and considerable compromise, the husband, wife, and each of the children defined the number of rooms, most desirable floor plan, ideal neighborhood, and many special features. Their need for the house was immediate (the family had grown), but the press of everyday life had caused them to delay their plans many times. Finally, they could wait no longer.

The husband considered himself a handyman and he was in fact good with tools. He had finished the basement and even put an addition on the family's existing house. The wife could also swing a hammer, but was more interested in specifying what she wanted. The kids (being kids) tried to help, but generally just got in the way. The family had three options:

1. They could buy an existing house. It would have the right number of rooms, but probably not the special features nor the exact floor plan they wanted.
2. They could contract the construction of the house to a third party—a general contractor who built houses for a living. They would get exactly what they wanted (plans and a contract would be established), but they would pay a twenty percent premium for the contractor's services.
3. They could build the house themselves, using a few vendors (like plumbers and electricians) to help in specialized areas. This would save money, and they'd get exactly what they wanted.

"Let's buy a house that's already built," said the wife. "We might not get everything we want, but we'll know the price going in and we'll be able to move in immediately."

"I don't like the idea of settling for something that doesn't really meet all of our needs," argued the husband. "Besides, we don't really know what we're getting, and our maintenance costs on an existing house may be high. What if we decide to make changes and find out that the construction behind the walls is shoddy?"

"Maybe," the wife replied, "but we've got a life to lead. You're not suggesting that we build the thing ourselves, are you?"

"Sure," responded the husband. "We can do it. And think of the money we'll save in the long run."

"I don't know," said the wife. "The family room took twice as long as we thought and the addition took us almost a year to complete when we thought it would take four months, and it cost a lot more than we expected. We could hire a contractor."

"Yeah, that's an option," said the husband. "Geez, I really don't know what to do."

"Neither do I," said the wife. "But I do know we better do something soon."

"We don't want to move anymore!" yelled the kids.

This vignette is about a family and their new house, or is it? Reread the paragraphs above and make the following substitutions:

Everywhere you encounter the word "family," substitute "business"; for "house," substitute "software." Wherever you encounter "husband" or "wife," substitute "engineering department" or "user"; for "children," substitute "management." Replace any reference to a house characteristic (like "number of rooms" or "floor plan") with a software characteristic.

Try it! What we've described above is a metaphor for the acquisition of software. The problems are the same, and the decisions are just as muddy.

Many companies and more and more individuals must acquire software on a regular basis. They all must decide whether to buy, build, or contract a software product to meet their needs. For some small businesses, for instance, the decision for a new accounting package may seem obvious at first, but it often turns out to be more complex. In the two chapters that follow, we focus on the issues to guide your choice and the ways to profit once the choice is made.

The Iron Age

9
To Buy or to Build
(or Maybe Both)

"Three years ago, I bought an Apple Macintosh computer," says the owner of a small advertising agency. "At first, I thought we'd use it for word processing, billing, that kind of thing.

"I obsessed about the decision to buy the computer because the hardware was pretty expensive. I figure we've spent about $8,000 buying the computer, a hard disk, a printer, and the like.

"Last week, one of my people asked me to buy another software package. It cost $395. It struck me that this one program represented five percent of what our computer cost. I looked back at our records, and you know what? We spent $9,350 on software since we bought the computer. The programs cost us more than the hardware!"

Software represents a substantial expense for anyone who uses computers. But before talking about buying, building, or contracting software, we need to review just what's out there. Thousands of applications programs have been created for hundreds of technology areas. Millions of people use these applications every day, and a nontrivial percentage asks for more. "If we just had" is the way most discussions begin, and they all converge on one of three software categories: We call them *custom, turnkey,* and *shrink-wrapped.*

Custom software is written for the specific needs of a small user community, typically an individual or group. Custom software can be acquired from a contractor or it can be developed by an in-house software engineering group within a company. (If you operate a small business or use computers for personal benefit, the in-house software engineering group may be you!) Regardless of its origin, custom software tends to be expensive to build and even more expensive to maintain.

Turnkey software is an existing product, and all the user has to do, at least in theory, is turn the key to use it. Sold in relatively small quantities and often tailored to the needs of each purchaser, turnkey applications typically cost tens of thousands of dollars, solve major business problems, and run on large as well as small computers. The supplier performs all of the maintenance and support for the application and distributes the costs of product development and maintenance among all customers. The customer gets a product that is focused on a specific business need (like bond portfolio analysis for banking) without the need for in-house computer expertise.

Shrink-wrapped software—the most recent addition to the software family—is purchased from a retail store shrink-wrapped in plastic. Retail cost is usually low because the developer distributes the cost of engineering and production over thousands or even hundreds of thousands of installations. Because shrink-wrapped software packages sell large numbers of copies, they are generic in nature. However, this enables developers to devote considerable effort to features that allow the end user to tailor the applications software. For example, many spreadsheets, databases, and graphics programs contain built-in programming facilities so that users can modify the functions to suit their purposes.

After reading the description of each software category, you might decide the choice is obvious: Buy shrink-wrapped software. After all, it's cheap, it solves many generic business problems, it can be customized to some extent, and it's as close as your local software store. This may be true for many situations, but only if you're doing computing-in-the-small—situations in which you intend to

- use stand-alone personal computers not connected in networks
- share little information created by the software among different staff members or other business applications
- process relatively small amounts of data at relatively low speed

Most individuals' requirements and many business situations fit this profile nicely. When they don't, you are forced to select from one of the other software categories.

The cost, adaptability to changing business needs, and specialization (the amount it is tailored to the function of a particular industry) of each software category varies dramatically. Custom software scores high in every category because it is written to the specifications of a single user or company and can be adapted to any situation (provided you are willing to pay the price). If you are looking for lower cost, but require limited specialization for your particular industry or business, the turnkey approach is a more attractive choice. Shrink-wrapped software offers the most attractive price, but won't be tailored to your specific business needs. Shrink-wrapped vendors are actually quite responsive about questions on the use of their packages and will help you to work around generic problems, but don't expect much guidance with something unique to your world.

There is one more very important criterion that we haven't mentioned in your decision: Time is often as important as cost, adaptability, and specialization. "If we buy, we save time," argue the proponents of the buy decision. "We can buy the software package and have it running tomorrow." This may in fact be true, but it can also be a mirage, as we'll see below.

It All Begins with a Simple Purchase

Joe Emerson is the owner of a small bookstore in a suburban community outside Chicago. Under pressure from the large chains, he decided to computerize the business to be more responsive to his customers and more competitive. Joe is a conservative businessman.

"I know very little about computers, so I studied the trade journals for suggestions," said Emerson. "I decided that BookZap 1.1 would be just the thing we needed for our type of business."

Armed with this information, Emerson contacted his local computer store. After lengthy discussions (much of which he really didn't understand), the salesperson convinced him to purchase a PC, hard disk, printer, and related equipment so that he could use BookZap 1.1 to its best advantage. For just over $7,000, Joe Emerson was set to join the computer revolution.

"When I took everything out of the boxes, I had my first pang of anxiety," smiles Joe. "But the computer was actually fairly simple to put together."

The two-inch thick manual describing the care of the computer was more than Joe had time to read. Being a good manager, he delegated responsibility for the computer to his assistant, Cary Davidson.

"I realized pretty quickly that the manuals for the PC and BookZap were not the best," recalls Davidson. "I asked Joe to send me to a training course at the computer store. He wasn't thrilled—it cost $350—but we really didn't have any other choice."

Once Cary had been trained, she wanted to computerize everything. Over the next six months, Cary convinced Joe that the store couldn't do without a variety of shrink-wrapped application packages. During this time, Cary struggled with BookZap 1.1 and finally had the program working.

"At about that time, I received a new version of the PC operating system," Davidson said. "The computer store said it fixed a lot of the problems with the older version, so we installed it at our store. Unfortunately, BookZap 1.1 didn't work with the new operating system, so we had to order an upgrade, version 1.2. It only cost $95."

In no time, the store became dependent on BookZap, inventories were easier to control, and customers got their orders filled more rapidly. Cary was now spending so much time with the computer that Joe hired a part-time assistant to perform her sales activities.

"Computers are funny," Joe smiled. "Once you see what they can do, you always want more. I asked Cary to generate special reports from BookZap to help us understand our middle-level sellers without having to wade through all the figures produced in a single month."

"It couldn't be done the way Joe wanted it," said Cary. "So I suggested we pay a few thousand dollars to a contract programmer who worked out of the computer store. He could build an interface that would translate BookZap reports into files for our spreadsheet. Then we could take the data from the spreadsheet and use it as input to our chart generation program. Joe would have a neat summary chart."

The programmer was hired and the interface project began. The results were so successful that Joe saw a business opportunity: He decided to sell the customized BookZap system and the homegrown summaries to fellow members of the Small Booksellers Trade Association. BookStore, Joe's new product, was well received. But since distribution and training grew to be too much for Cary to handle alone, a support staff was hired to handle the load. The contract programmer then could spend full-time supervising a new local area network and supporting remote telecommunications. Despite some start-up difficulties, the system eventually came on-line and business flowed smoothly again.

"We were really cooking," said Cary, now the manager of software activities, "until disaster struck."

The programmer of the interface that made BookStore a success left for bluer skies. "I'm burnt out," he lamented as he packed his bags for Hawaii.

A few weeks later, a package arrived on Cary's desk. It was BookZap 3.0, touted as "the answer to every user's needs." Unfortunately, this version's input formats were different from the previous versions. Consequently, BookStore wouldn't work with the new version of BookZap.

"I wasn't particularly worried," remembers Cary. "I knew that a new contact programmer worked for the computer store, so I gave him a call. After one look at our existing interface programs, he told me major modifications would be required and it would cost two and a half times what the original cost us."

"That's where we are right now," scowls Joe. "What if I pay for this change and then some other program within BookStore changes or what if this new whizbang product makes BookStore obsolete and we have to start all over again?"

Welcome to the world of software, Joe.

We could continue the tale of the initiation of Joe and Cary, but for some readers it may already be too painful (and too close to home). Therefore, we'll stop to draw some conclusions from this story.

- Software's original purchase price is usually minor compared to the other costs.
- Operating computer systems requires dedicated, responsible personnel.
- Training of personnel can be a significant cost.

- Successful application of software in one area will lead to additional applications in other areas.
- Purchased software will need to be updated periodically and this cost is paid in either update or maintenance fees.

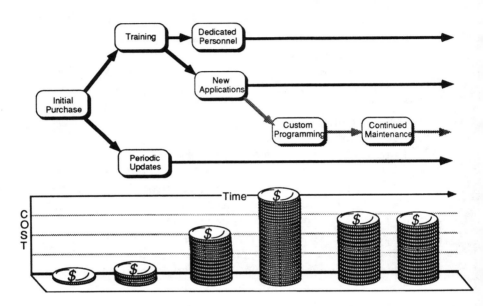

There is more to the cost of using computer software than the initial purchase price of a package.

- Each new software application usually requires some form of interfacing to existing applications. Custom programming for this purpose is very expensive.
- Once some custom programming is included in a system, it will require continual maintenance.
- Continuous change in the software environment and the costs associated with it are inevitable. This situation will not change for the foreseeable future.

There's another lesson if you read between the lines: Even when you intend only to buy software, you may ultimately wind up building or contracting it as well. Faced with this list of costs, many people become wary of acquiring software. Let us consider each of the costs for possible ways to ease the burden.

- *Original purchase price:* Don't worry too much about this; it will be minor in the long run.
- *Personnel:* Start by acquiring programs that do not need dedicated support; if support becomes necessary (and it often does), try to find the right person for the job and budget for it.
- *Training:* Balance this cost against the advantages gained and remember that ignorance always costs more in the long run.
- *Success breeds success:* That's good, not bad, but be sure you aren't lulled into the misdirected assumption that because the first application worked out so well, the next one will too.
- *Updates:* Don't be tempted into the if-it's-not-broke-don't-fix-it mindset that causes you to forego updates. After a while, your software will no longer be supported and may no longer operate when other changes occur.
- *Applications interfacing:* Look for applications that don't require much interfacing. Avoid custom programming whenever possible.
- *Custom programming maintenance:* Plan for this as an ongoing expense similar to building repairs or replacement of equipment.
- *Continuous change:* Anticipate change; prepare for the danger and exploit the opportunities.

After considering each of these issues, you are ready to balance the advantages of information technology against the inevitable costs. The story of Joe Emerson's bookstore is relatively common, but it need not be your story. A wise decision maker simply needs to keep all of the facts in mind.

The NIH Syndrome

The buy, build, or contract decision is frequently influenced more by ego than by common sense. In a technology company, as in many others as well, ego manifests itself in the *Not Invented Here* syndrome. NIH frequently appears when the buy, build, or contract decision for software is discussed. Regardless of how well targeted, how reliable, and how inexpensive a turnkey or shrink-wrapped program is, it can never be good enough for those people who didn't build it themselves.

> We once sat in on a meeting with the software marketing and the engineering managers of a major computer company, who argued over acquiring a software product of a small start-up company.
>
> "Look," the marketing manager said acidly, "the beta version of this software will be available in a month. It does everything we need and fits our plans perfectly. And you're telling me that Software Engineering can't get a similar product done for at least fifteen months."
>
> "You're going to walk off a cliff," warned the engineering manager. "How do we control this product, how do we support it, how do we extend it? We have to build it internally so we can provide reasonable answers to those questions."
>
> "The market doesn't care about those questions, at least not right now—they want product," answered the marketing manager, becoming more than a little agitated. "Look, we could buy the damned start-up if you have trouble with the control issue. Then the technology is ours for keeps."
>
> "It still wouldn't be ours—we didn't build it!" countered the engineering manager.

There may have been some validity to the engineering manager's concerns, but it was reasonably obvious that he suffered from a severe case of NIH syndrome. What happened? The company built its own version of the software and missed the market window.

The problem with NIH is that it leads to illogical decision making. If a company must build everything itself, there is significant and often unnecessary expense, substantial and often avoidable time delay, and an overburdened development staff. The following scenario frequently signals the onset of software-related NIH syndrome:

- An important internal need can be met by software available from a third party.
- Software developers outline an in-house (custom) approach to meet the need.
- The customer/users want a solution "now."
- The developers grudgingly agree to consider the third-party solution.
- After a cursory look at the product, the developers reject it (often on trumped-up charges).
- Management and/or the customer/users—goaded by salespeople from the third party—insist on a more detailed evaluation. They are intoxicated with the promise of instant delivery.
- The developers build an assessment matrix, a set of criteria to compare the outside solution to the internally developed program. (Note: The assessment matrix is usually loaded in favor of in-house development.)
- The detailed assessment comes to the same conclusion: Build in-house. Customers/users are disappointed. Management is confused.
- NIH lurks in the background.

Most managers and employees will agree intellectually that NIH is not an effective way to run a business. Unfortunately, ego is not an intellectual problem, but an emotional one. To overcome NIH, software developers must somehow feel they own the software, even if they didn't build it. They must be involved in its selection, must work to customize it to their own needs, and must interact with the vendor to build in-house expertise.

The BWC Syndrome

A distant but equally dangerous cousin of NIH is the *But We Can't* syndrome. You can spot this malady every time a new worthwhile idea, product, or technology is proposed and someone says, "But we can't because

- we can't afford it.
- it's too radical.
- we've never done it before.
- we're too big.
- we're too small.
- we're too conservative.
- management will never buy it.

The ultimate in negative thinking, BWC strikes managers and technologists alike, for trying something new entails risk. Change is hard.

Whenever BWC appears in the decision making process, creativity is the victim. Akio Morita, the Chairman of Sony Corporation, co-authored the controversial book *"No" to ieru Nihon (The Japan That Can Say No),* which has reportedly sold more than a million copies in Japan. Intended exclusively for a Japanese readership, it discusses Japan's emerging role as a world superpower and its relationship with the United States. To quote an informal translation:

> Industry requires three types of creativity. The first, of course, is the basic creativity necessary to make technological inventions and

discoveries. [Morita praises the U.S. in this category.] This alone, however, does not make for good business or good industry.

The second type of creativity that is necessary is that involving how to use this new technology, and how to use it in large quantities and in a manner that is appropriate. In English, this would be called "product planning and production creativity."

The third type of creativity is in marketing. That is, selling things you have produced. Even if you succeed in manufacturing something, it takes marketing to put that article to actual use before you have a business.

The strength in Japanese industry is in finding many ways of turning basic technology into products and in using basic technology. In basic technology, it is true that Japan has relied on foreign sources. Turning technology into products is where Japan is number one in the world.[*]

Whether we talk about technology in general or software in particular, BWC affects all of the categories described by Morita. One of the reasons that Japanese business has been so successful in recent decades is its willingness to be creative. The Japanese rarely succumb to BWC.

Sometimes, the amount of BWC encountered at technical and management levels seems directly proportional to company size. Small, entrepreneurial companies rarely suffer from the syndrome, but larger, more bureaucratic companies often do. People with vision, with guts, with drive, with charisma, never suffer from BWC.

In an unusual twist, software people tend to apply BWC to themselves. When asked to change or try something new, they sometimes respond:

---

[*]We obtained this controversial translation of the book when it appeared on the Internet network. Because of the controversy, Morita has resisted English translation of the book in its original form. His co-author Shintaro Ishihara has written a version of the book without Morita's remarks. The complete reference is S. Ishihara, *The Japan That Can Say No,* trans. F. Baldwin (New York: Simon & Schuster, 1991).

- "But we can't learn that method, it'll take too long."
- "But we can't use that tool, it won't work here."
- "But we can't spend time defining what we need to do, we're already late."

The danger of BWC thinking is that people will reject ideas before they have the facts. When software managers are asked to manage change and to commit resources to effect change, they may say:

- "But we can't afford to train staff, project deadlines will slip."
- "But we can't get them tools, they're expensive."

The BWC syndrome occurs when people make decisions using a value set that is no longer valid. For example, software developers thought for many years that the user had to contort to meet the interaction needs of the computer. IBM, Digital Equipment Corp., Hewlett-Packard, and a dozen other computer giants said "But we can't" when asked for user-friendly software interfaces. Then, along came Apple Computer and the Macintosh, and the world of interface software was changed forever.

After the BWC syndrome is overcome, people are free to explore new ideas. Although adoption of new ideas may be difficult at first, they often result in new efficiencies, new capabilities, and new products.

Should software people avoid BWC in every instance? Of course not. If the facts indicate that going forward would be unwise, "We choose not to" is a valid conclusion.

A converse syndrome that is just as debilitating is *We Can Do Anything*. This occurs when people try too hard to please and make commitments they can't possibly keep. A single successful project can make software folks quite cocky, resulting in WCDA.

NIH and WCDA can overlap when software developers grapple with the buy versus build dilemma. Applying NIH, they first reject any outside source of software, and then applying WCDA, they believe they can build a better version in an unrealistically short time.

The Maintenance Trap

Hamilton Cash is the engineering manager for a medium size company that builds sophisticated measurement equipment for industrial quality control. The equipment costs well over $100,000 and is customized to each customer's needs. The company's premier product—the MET-1—is a microprocessor-based measurement system with more than sixty thousand lines of code embedded within it.

"We really had no choice but to build the programs ourselves," says Cash. "After all, it's the software that gives us a competitive advantage. A few of our people wanted to contract it out, but that never went anywhere. Software was new to us, but we learned to build it."

"You don't look happy with the current situation," we responded.

"The problem is that every MET-1 is delivered with slightly different software in it—no two are exactly alike. We've kept informal records of which customers have which versions of the software, but we're really out of control. When we make a change to the baseline software, we can't just send it out to our customers because we can't be sure that it won't create a problem with something unique to their system. One of our field service people has to hand-deliver the software, figure out what version the customer has, and then install the update."

When asked how this approach is working out, Cash's face tightens, "Not well, in fact, it's an absolute nightmare.

"Updates never seem to work the first time they're installed. Our customers are screaming because their machines are down. There have been a few times when we've had to call a customer and ask what version of the software they had. They asked how come we didn't know. Moves like that don't inspire confidence."

Hamilton Cash stares out his office window, as if looking for an answer. "When we began building software, no one realized the impact of software maintenance. We fell into a trap and it's going to take some real effort to get out."

Whenever software is built, there is an implicit commitment: The builder makes a commitment to correct errors, to provide updates, to adapt the program to changes in its environment. The builder becomes a maintainer and, in so doing, commits to years or even decades of continuing work on an existing computer program.

For many software builders (particularly those new to the game), the magnitude of this commitment comes as a shock. Technical staffs rapidly lose their enthusiasm for maintenance, wishing instead to do something new. Management becomes weary of the maintenance burden, wishing that there was a way to reduce the resource drain. Customers demand the commitment, but are rarely satisfied with what they get.

There appears to be an easy escape from the maintenance trap: Why not buy or contract software instead of building it? The burden of maintenance would therefore fall on the software vendor or the software contractor.

Unfortunately, the escape is not so easy. Relying on a third party for software maintenance of an existing product puts you at their mercy. Errors can go uncorrected for weeks or months. Enhancements may take months or even years to get (and only then if they have broad market appeal). Adaptations for a new computer or operating system are made at the pleasure of the vendor.

When you buy, assume that what you see is what you get. New versions of the product will be provided (if you are willing to pay for them), but the time frame and direction are outside your control.

In some cases, custom software contracting provides a better maintenance solution. Since the contractor builds a program to your exact specifications, these people should be able to maintain what they built, right? Maybe. The contractor can encounter the same maintenance problems as a software builder, if good software engineering practices have not been followed. Even if good practices have been used, some contractors refuse to do maintenance after an initial break-in period, turning the burden over to the purchaser. Those contractors willing to perform maintenance activities indefinitely recognize the costs associated with software maintenance and demand a high price for doing it.

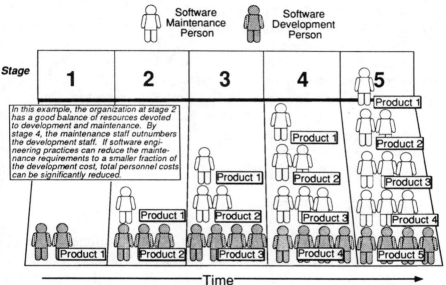

Although new software products require considerable investment, it is the ongoing maintenance costs that are most significant in the long run. Good software engineering practices can help to control maintenance costs.

The maintenance trap is set. If you build, you'll incur the direct cost of performing maintenance yourself. If you buy, you'll be at the mercy of the vendor, waiting for corrections, adaptations, and enhancements and having virtually no control over their frequency or relevance to your work. If you contract, you may still be burdened with maintenance, or you'll pay a steep price to have it performed for you.

Is there a way to avoid the trap? Only if you proceed with care and recognize there is no free lunch. Carefully examine the existing software product to be sure you can live with it, as is, into the foreseeable future. If you can't, you probably need to look for an alternate solution.

Be absolutely sure that good software engineering practices have been applied, no matter who builds the software. Properly engineered software will exhibit characteristics of order and simplicity that start deep inside and go beyond, even to the instruction manual and the user interface.

Make sure that good documentation describes the product. Ask the vendor about the frequency and dates of new releases. If these questions can't be answered, it is a prelude to trouble. Discuss maintenance issues with contractors before the contract is signed; understand the costs. Above all, recognize that the cost of the original computer program may be small indeed, when compared to the long-term cost of maintaining it.

Buying It, Then Building It

Sometimes the answer to the buy versus build dilemma can be solved by using an existing software product as a model for building your own custom version. In essence, the existing software product serves as a prototype for the system that you intend to build. This is an especially good approach if you do not know how to get started or if you need a solution immediately. This approach is like buying a mobile home to live in on your land while you build your dream house from the ground up.

Building It, Then Buying It

In organizations devoted exclusively to research and development, building it, then buying it can be useful. If the research goal is unclear but the perceived benefit substantial, there is often merit in building a prototype of the desired software. Through an iterative process of brainstorming, experimentation, and testing, an R&D organization can refine a new idea into a new product design. Once a successful prototype is built and evaluated, it may be more practical to turn over the construction of the final product to an outside contractor. Alternatively, the prototype may be licensed to another company that will build and market a product based on the prototype (that is, build it yourself, then buy it back). This approach is similar to architects who build many models of a house. When they find one they like, a building contractor is hired to construct the dwelling in its final form.

Last Thoughts

There is no magic formula for determining which type of software will address the needs of a particular individual or organization. Usually, custom software will give the greatest level of adaptability for business needs, but its cost will be the highest. This does not mean that custom software should be rejected as an option. A lower-cost solution that doesn't solve the problem is worse than no solution at all. Frequently, the answer is to choose a turnkey or shrink-wrapped application and then budget for some level of customization to address specific needs. If you choose to buy vanilla applications and add your own toppings to them, remember that customization is an expensive activity.

If you conclude that vendor-supplied software must be customized, be aware that most turnkey and shrink-wrapped vendors provide some built-in programmability within their systems. Customization using this approach is often less expensive and certainly less risky than becoming mired in the maintenance trap.

Planned Obsolescence

10
Software and You: How to Profit

To see who was the smartest, an engineer, a business person, and a mathematician decided to take a simple test. The object of the test was to boil water. Each person was to enter two different rooms. In the first room, a pot of water and a box of matches sat on a table beside a small gas stove. In the second room, a pot of water rested on the floor, and a box of matches sat on a table beside a gas stove.

Upon entering the first room, all the participants performed identically. They each entered the room, evaluated the situation, and then picked up the pot of water from the table, placed it on the burner of the stove, lit a fire using the matches, and waited for the water to boil.

In the second room, they each performed differently. The engineer entered the room, evaluated the situation, and then picked up the pot of water from the floor, placed it on the table, and then executed the sequence of steps that she learned in the first room. The business person entered the room, evaluated the situation, and then, recognizing that the water was heavy and that lifting it to the table would be difficult, left to find someone to hire to do the job. The mathematician entered the room, evaluated the situation, and then picked up the pot of water from the floor, placed it on the table and left, never to return. He had reduced the situation to a problem that had already been solved.

What if the test were different? What if the engineer, the business person, and the mathematician were asked to develop a strategy for taking advantage of the opportunities offered by software in the years ahead? How would they each approach the task?

The engineer would learn everything she could about software, building on past knowledge and performing all of the technical chores herself. This is an excellent way to proceed, provided there is sufficient background, time, and resources. The business person would recognize immediately that a detailed understanding of the technology is not necessary to its use. As long as the potential is understood, most of the technology can be purchased, subcontracted, or delegated to some other person or organization. The mathematician's approach would be that of a computer science researcher, who studies areas of potential opportunity, but doesn't necessarily pursue them to a practical end.

Which of these three approaches is best? Each has merit in its own right, but the most realistic approach for benefiting from the opportunities offered by software is to combine elements of all three.

A Simple Strategy

Software represents the means for tapping the enormous potential of modern computers, and those who do will become more productive, more responsive, and more creative.

How do you tap the potential? Should you be an engineer, a business person, a mathematician, all three, or something else entirely? The answer lies in applying a simple three-step strategy:

1. Learn enough about software technology so that you can make intelligent choices (reading this book is a good start).
2. Select an area of opportunity in your work or daily life and investigate how software can help make you more productive.
3. Choose one or more of the many existing software packages that have been developed to meet your needs.

To learn about the technology, begin by obtaining a general understanding of computers and software. Most large corporations have training courses available for employees at all levels. Colleges, universities, and adult education programs offer a wide variety of courses in many different aspects of software. Local community colleges and computer retail stores offer training programs for frequently used personal computer software.

If you prefer less structured learning, there are literally thousands of tutorials available in the form of books and videotape. Professional organizations of all types offer seminars and workshops on software related to a specific area of expertise. The array of software-related books that appear in the "Computers" section of the average bookstore is surprisingly large. You only need to scratch around a little to turn up a myriad of educational opportunities.

Once you feel comfortable with the subject as a whole, you have to focus a bit. Begin by understanding the generic classes of computer programs that are relevant to your world. Create a taxonomy by building a generic hierarchy of program classes that are relevant to your work or your life. For example, if you feel that business applications on the PC offer potential, build a taxonomy like this:

business software:
> word processing
>> word processing packages
>> grammar checking
>> spell checking
>> envelope/label printing
>
> desktop publishing
>> page layout and design
>> graphics art
>> font design and management
>
> graphics and drawing
>> simple line drawing packages
>> sophisticated color graphics

spreadsheets
database management
        record-oriented databases
        mailing lists
        multimedia databases
communications
        modem/communications management
        file conversion
financial
        general ledger
        accounts payable/receivable
        billing
time management
        calendars
        appointment books

Although only a partial list, this taxonomy would serve most business people well. Next, learn a bit about each generic class (see the next section for suggestions).

Once you feel comfortable with software technology basics, isolate areas of opportunity or leverage applications. That is, examine those areas in your work and daily life where you spend the most time. Is there an opportunity to automate some portion of the activity? If you think not, look for activities that you don't particularly enjoy, that waste your time, or that you view as drudgery. There may be opportunities here that you've overlooked.

Once you've identified an area, break it into substeps to determine whether software can be used. For example, if you spend substantial time writing, a word processing or desktop publishing software would benefit you. Further analysis of the writing activity might reveal that the following tasks are performed every day:

• reading magazines to find useful quotes and information
• doing simple computations with relevant statistics

- writing a draft document
- editing the document to improve style
- proofreading the document
- illustrating your writing with pictures or graphs

This exercise identified at least six software opportunities, and they all are being met by shrink-wrapped software for the PC, including a database system, a spreadsheet, a conventional word processing package, a grammar/style checker, a spelling checker, and a drawing program.

Before you choose any area, you can better understand the potential opportunities by creating a list of daily tasks and a taxonomy of the software applications that address these tasks.

The Problem of Choices

Although this strategy seems reasonable enough, there is a problem: the problem of choices. Once you have isolated an area of opportunity, you may find there are dozens or even hundreds of software packages that (on the surface, at least) seem to meet your needs. How should you choose? Here are some options:

Don't worry about choices—just do it. Choose the first product you find and hope for the best. This is not as irrational or random as it seems, especially if the software application you are considering is mature, like word processing or spreadsheets. In these areas, any product on the market will do the job adequately. Though your choice may not meet your every requirement, any choice will provide some benefit. If, however, the applications area is new, market feedback has not yet been integrated into subsequent improved software versions and the package chosen at random may be of questionable quality and utility.

Research the literature. A plethora of magazines cover PC software products, which are often rated against a comprehensive set of criteria, including those you might not have considered. Published comparisons help you to understand what's important and what to look for in the software that you need. Software products that score high in the rating are obviously good candidates for purchase.

Scan software product catalogs published by direct mail retailers. Spend a few hours each month thumbing through direct mail catalogs for software. Most have brief descriptions of new and old software products categorized by applications area (use your taxonomy as a guide).

Go to your local computer or software store. Knowledgeable salespeople can often provide guidance once you've defined your requirements, but the advice you receive may be based on limited experience and a less-than-objective assessment of the available products.

Join a local computer group to find someone with similar needs as yours. By asking someone who's already made the decision, you'll learn about product features that really count, and equally important, those that don't. A firsthand recommendation for a software product is ideal.

Join an electronic conference service. Most electronic information services, like Compuserve, have a wide array of electronic conferences and information forums dedicated to specific software applications areas, and sometimes even to specific products. You can eavesdrop by reading the comments posted, or you can take a more active role.

Selecting one or more of these options helps solve the problem of choices, and you'll eventually select a program that meets your needs and achieves its primary goal—to make you more productive, more responsive, and more creative. But even with good research and the best strategy, you will occasionally select a software clunker that just doesn't perform as advertised. When you do, don't continue to use it just because you've spent the money. Admit your error and choose a product that will do the job.

The Road to Sophistication

So the choice is made. Will the software product result in immediate productivity improvement or an instantaneous jolt in creativity? Not likely. First you'll have to evolve through these stages of sophistication:

Learner. You've loaded the new software into your machine and are ready to go. Maybe you've spent a few minutes reading the manual (and maybe not). The best products allow you to explore while at the same time learn the mechanics of using them. This learning stage is completed only after you can perform the most basic operations and use the product to do something useful, even if it is very simple.

Novice. You use the program on a regular basis. With each session, you recognize the need to learn a bit more about the mechanics of usage, and this you do. You're making fewer silly mistakes and you're producing useful, albeit basic, output that provides some benefit to you and/or your colleagues.

Experienced user. You are now comfortable with the program, as you move efficiently through it and understand its rhythm. You are more productive as a result.

Expert. You are a power user. You use the program to its fullest, knowing even the most obscure features of the software. You eagerly await new versions of the program that will remedy failings that are obvious to you. You create information that makes your life much easier. You are the one whom others come to with questions.

How long does it take to travel along the road to sophistication? Your evolution from learner to expert may take a week or it may never happen. The speed with which you travel and the distance that you move along the road will have much to do with your own skills and motivation, the amount of time you spend with the software, and the complexity of the tasks that you are asked to perform.

The Road to Knowledge*

The road to sophistication is also the road to knowledge. But here we're not talking about an in-depth knowledge of the software application. Rather, we mean an increase in your knowledge that will increase your productivity, save your time, or enhance your creativity. But how can this be? After all, these characteristics depend on a person, not a computer program. The answer lies in software's ability to transform data into information and information into knowledge.

Over the past two decades, a subtle transition has occurred in the terminology used to describe software work performed for the business community. Twenty years ago, the term data processing was the operative phrase for describing the use of computers in a business context. Today, data processing has given way to another phrase—information technology—that implies the same thing but presents a subtle shift in focus. The emphasis is not merely to process large quantities of data, but rather to extract meaningful information from this data. Obviously, this was always the intent, but the shift in terminology reflects a revised outlook on how one can profit from software.

Data is raw information—collections of facts that must be processed to be meaningful. Information is derived by associating facts within a given context. Knowledge assimilates information obtained in one context and associates it with other information obtained in a different context. Finally, wisdom occurs when generalized principles are derived from disparate knowledge.

To date, the vast majority of all software has been built to process data and thereby create useful information. Software engineers of the twenty-first century will be equally concerned with systems

---

*This section is adapted from R. Pressman's *Software Engineering: A Practitioner's Approach,* 3rd ed. (New York: McGraw-Hill, 1992), with permission of the publisher.

that process knowledge. Knowledge is two-dimensional. Information collected on a variety of related and unrelated topics is connected to form a body of facts that we call knowledge. The key is our ability to associate information from a variety of different sources that may not have any obvious connection to one another and combine it in a way that provides us with some distinct benefit.

To illustrate the progression from data to knowledge, consider recent census data indicating that the birthrate in 1990 in the United States was 4.1 million. This number represents a data value. Relating this piece of data to birthrates for the preceding forty years, we can derive a useful piece of information: Aging baby boomers of the 1950s are having children just prior to the end of their childbearing years. We can connect this piece of information to other seemingly unrelated pieces of information, for example, the current number of elementary school teachers who will retire during the next decade; the number of college students graduating with degrees in primary and secondary education; and the pressure on politicians to hold down taxes and therefore limit pay increases for teachers.

Each of these pieces of information can be combined to formulate a representation of knowledge—there will be significant pressure on the education system in the U.S. in the late 1990s and this pressure will continue for over a decade. Armed with this knowledge, you may have the opportunity to profit. For instance, you might start a company that develops new modes of learning that are more effective and less costly than current approaches.

The Road to Creativity

The road to knowledge has many lanes and one of them leads to creativity. Knowledge extracted from business information can enhance the creativity of a business person. Suddenly, a trend becomes obvious, an opportunity becomes apparent, a hidden pitfall becomes visible. The insight provided by software enables the user to respond in creative fashion. The software magnifies the user's creativity by accentuating those pieces of information that are relevant to the user's needs.

But what of nonbusiness or nontechnical situations? What if raw data have little direct bearing on your work? Is it possible, for example, for software to enhance the creativity of an artist, a musician, a writer? We think the answer is yes.

Like any good tool, software magnifies the abilities of its user. If the user is unskilled, software may help a bit, but it won't produce highly creative work. However, if the user is skilled, the magnification factor is significant—that is, software magnifies the creativity of a skilled user to a much greater extent than it affects an unskilled user.

Although many purists in the arts continue to shun the computer (and therefore discount the impact of software), others are beginning to recognize that software is a tool for enhanced creativity. The artist can use computer graphics, artificial reality systems, and sophisticated video augmentation to create forms of art that were unknown just ten years ago. The musician can use software to compose, to capture nonmusical sounds for incorporation into music, to synthesize new sounds, and to produce the result recorded on digital compact disks or digital tape. The writer uses word processing, spelling and grammar checking, and an on-line thesaurus to produce written material more quickly and accurately. The ability to modify easily enables writers to tune their work for greatest impact.

The Road to Tomorrow

If modern society profits from computer software, it will be because each of us—the business person and the technologist, the factory worker and the artist, the student and the teacher—has captured the information that software produces and has used it to improve our personal knowledge and creativity. We face significant opportunities and frightening dangers as we approach the twenty-first century.

Everyone, in his or her own way, must overcome software shock so that we will have the creativity (and courage) to prevail.

Our journey together is finished. If your imagination has been captured, and you are inspired to explore the world of software further, we are pleased. If your knowledge and understanding of computer software have increased, we have accomplished our mission. You may be startled by the rapid changes that lie ahead, but you will no longer suffer from software shock.

Glossary

ad hoc approach: an approach to writing code and building software systems without first creating a design and establishing requirements, standards, and procedures to be followed. Analogous to building a house without any blueprints.

algorithm: a formal procedure for any mathematical operation.

analyst: a software person who is a problem solver, who communicates and consults with customers, and who suggests how technology can be applied to solve their problem.

appliance computer: a ready-to-run computer typically acquired from a retail store. Its design and instructions assume that the user will set up and begin to use it without the help or advice of computing support personnel.

applications backlog: the accumulation of unfilled requests for software products.

applications software: software designed for a specific purpose to fill a particular need such as payroll processing, drafting, or inventory control.

apprentice: a junior staff member who works under the tutelage of a sorcerer.

artificial intelligence: the controversial term for the application of computers and software to tasks that when performed by humans would be construed to involve intelligence.

artificial reality: a simulation of reality or proposed reality created using computer technology, such that people can experience this unreal world with all of their senses (also known as virtual reality).

assessment matrix: a set of criteria that an organization can use to compare third-party solutions with internally developed programs to decide which solution would best satisfy business needs.

attending engineer: a software engineer with enough general knowledge to insure the program survives the ministrations of software specialists.

authoring system: the part of courseware enabling the creation of mixed media presentations to bring educational information to students; ideally designed for use by an educator, not a computing specialist.

bandwidth: a term borrowed from electronics, meaning the range of radio frequencies in a band. In computing, it refers to the volume of information that can be passed through a hardware or software component.

bathtub curve: a failure rate curve characteristic of new hardware, beginning with a high failure rate, then dropping and rising again as components begin to wear out.

bug: a defect in software that causes it to fail to perform its function under certain circumstances; humorously referred to as "an undocumented restriction."

business product: a prepackaged, ready-to-use software product designed to address business needs; normally designed to be used as is (as opposed to being customized).

CD-ROM: the acronym for compact disc read only memory. Uses the same technology as the audio industry to store information for computer use. Especially attractive because the CD-ROM is easy and inexpensive to reproduce, while holding huge quantities of information.

chief information officer (CIO): a new term for a corporate officer responsible for software use and development throughout a corporation. Analogous to the chief financial officer or chief executive officer.

code: the instructions that make up a program.

coding: the writing and entering of code/instructions; an early term for programming.

complex system: a set of software and hardware components that synthesizes information in ways that would be virtually impossible to do manually.

computer-aided design (CAD): a collection of software tools used by engineers and architects that allows them to develop detailed design schematics, then to view and modify them easily and rapidly.

computer-aided engineering (CAE): a collection of software tools used by engineers that allows them to perform engineering design analysis that is beyond what could be practically done using manual methods. Usually involves some aspects of computer-aided design (CAD).

computer-aided manufacturing (CAM): a collection of software tools used to control and monitor manufacturing processes. Frequently used in conjunction with computer-aided design and computer-aided engineering, hence the term CADAM (computer-aided design and manufacturing).

computer-aided software engineering (CASE): a variety of software tools that aid software engineers in the design and development process by automating many manual activities.

computer-based system/products: any set of activities or functions that depend heavily upon computers and their associated software.

computer graphics: the pictorial presentation of information and ideas using computer hardware and software technology.

computer-integrated manufacturing (CIM): also called flexible manufacturing, it is software that enables computers to control the manufacturing process by coordinating the machinery, raw materials, and personnel. A successor to CAM.

consumer product: a prepackaged (shrink-wrapped) software product designed for use by an individual on a personal computer.

contractor: a supplier of software under an outside contract.

courseware: interactive educational software that can be customized to accommodate many learning modes by presenting information in a variety of different ways.

customer: the person or group who has a problem to be solved, attempts to define the problem, and uses the software product created and built to solve the problem (refers to an individual, organizational entity, or market segment).

customer support group: the group in a software development organization responsible for helping customers and users solve problems with their software. They serve as an intermediary between the customer and the company.

custom product: a product specifically designed and implemented according to a customer's requirements.

custom software: computer programs developed for the specific needs of a user and typically acquired from a contractor or developed by an in-house software engineering group at a high cost.

database: a collection of data organized in such a way that the data can be searched, retrieved, and assembled as related information.

data processing: a dated term describing the use of computers in a business context; currently being replaced by "information technology," a term that implies a subtle shift in focus from data to information.

debugging: the process of testing a program to find errors and removing the source of the errors.

desktop computer: a self-contained computer system small enough to fit on top of an ordinary desk.

ease of use: the property of a computer program that anticipates the user's needs, guides the user through difficult procedures, protect the users from making an error, and controls the impact of any mistake that does slip through.

electronic commuting: the use of computer and telecommunications technology so that employees can accomplish their tasks remotely, without physically going to a business office.

electronic mail: a mail system in which messages are created, transmitted, stored, forwarded, and displayed by a network of computers.

embedded system: a set of software that offers advanced features and is included as part of a larger product (such as a microwave oven or an airplane).

end user: the person or group who directly interacts with a computer and the software.

engineering development group: the group in a software development organization responsible for the analysis and design necessary to integrate the software and hardware of a system (also called systems group).

expert system: computer software that has been programmed with a set of rules defined by a human expert. When presented with a problem, the expert system responds in the same manner as a human expert (also known as a knowledge-based system).

facsimile: the transmission and reproduction of written or graphic material by electronic means.

fiber optics: a communications technology that uses fibers for transmiting light to carry signals. Fiber optic cables can carry enormous volumes of information at relatively low costs.

fire fighter: a software person who responds to emergencies ranging from correcting bugs to adding functions to a software system.

fourth-generation language: the latest step in the evolution of programming languages. Involves significantly higher levels of abstraction than traditional procedural languages such as FORTRAN, COBOL, or BASIC.

FURPS: Hewlett-Packard-derived acronym of the attributes that measure the quality of a software product. They are functionality, usability, reliability, performance, and supportability.

future shock: a term coined by Alvin Toffler "to describe the shattering stress and disorientation that we induce in individuals by subjecting them to too much change in too short a time."

gatekeeper: the person in a software development organization (often part of the product research group) who provides technical information and expertise to solve specific problems. Ideally, the person is knowledgeable about both the technology and the business of the company.

graphics: (*see* **computer graphics**)

graphic user interface (GUI): the technique for using computer graphics displays and an interactive pointing device such as a mouse to enhance the ease of use properties of a computer system and its software.

grunt: a member of a software development team who works under a sorcerer.

guru: (*see* **sorcerer**)

hacker: has multiple connotations, among them (1) a knowledgeable, creative programmer, (2) an information pirate who applies his/her skill and creativity to break into computer systems, (3) an undisciplined programmer who shuns the engineering approach to software development.

hardware: the physical components of a computer system.

high-resolution computer graphics: (*see* **resolution**)

human-computer interface: the mechanism by which software systems and their users communicate with each other. A recent trend is to shift the burden in this area from the user to the software.

industry-quality software: robust, reliable products that function well under difficult conditions.

information agent: an interface program that can perform a variety of data processing and clerical functions, and is customized to the users' needs; can be given human-like characteristics.

information revolution: a term that refers to the great change in how information and data are created, used, and communicated as a result of new technology.

information store: an electronic retail store of the future that sells information tailored to the preferences of an individual customer.

information technology: the use of computer hardware and software to facilitate the task of turning data into information. Replaces the older term "data processing" and implies greater emphasis on information than data.

integrated circuit: an electronic device made by etching many individual electronic components onto a single piece of semiconductor material such as silicon; today a single integrated circuit can do the work once performed by thousands of transistors. The remarkable progress made in the manufacturing of these devices over the past twenty years has been primarily responsible for the increasing power and declining cost of computer hardware.

intelligent assistant: the software that assists a user by anticipating needs or requests based on a stored profile of the individual's preferences and work habits.

intelligent machine: a machine controlled by software; rather than perform a single function, it acquires information from its environment and responds based on rules established by its controlling software.

interactive computing: the use of computer hardware and software in a manner that involves a dialogue between the applications software and the user. Considered common today, but less so in the 1960s when the large, expensive mainframes of that era usually performed their processing tasks isolated from user intervention.

interactive system: a set of computer programs that performs its functions by carrying on a dialogue with the end user.

interface: a connection of two or more things brought together in an association, partnership, meeting, or other relationship.

just-in-time strategy: an approach in which raw materials for production are carefully regulated so as to keep costs and inventories low; supplies are acquired as they are needed, thus eliminating the need to store them in inventory.

LED: the acronym for light emitting diode; a crystalline semiconducting device that glows with a bright light when current flows through it.

life cycle: progression of a software system from the initial problem definition through design, implementation, deployment, maintenance, and eventually replacement.

lights out factory: a completely automated factory that requires no people, just computers and machines.

machine code: instructions that can be directly interpreted by a computer; does not require any translation.

machine-dependent language statement: a component of a programming language that is dependent upon specific computer hardware.

mainframe computer: a large, powerful, and expensive computer system designed to serve many users; usually controlled and operated by a staff of computing professionals.

maintainer: the person responsible for making the corrections, adaptations, and enhancements of existing programs; a software archaeologist, who studies old programs in order to fix them.

maintenance: the process of error correction, adaptation, and enhancement of an existing product. In the software life cycle, it often entails making significant changes in the design of the product.

management by consensus: a management technique that borrows from the principles of democratic government and suggests that employee involvement leads to higher performance and stronger dedication to the corporate goals.

methodology: a system of methods or procedures used in developing software.

microprocessor: a single integrated circuit that contains all of the electronic components making up the central processing unit of a computer.

minicomputer: a medium-powered computer designed to serve a moderate number of users; usually controlled and operated by a smaller, less sophisticated staff than a mainframe computer.

modem: the acronym for **mo**dulator **dem**odulator, a device used in telecommunications to convert digital signals to analog form and vice versa; an apparatus that lets computers communicate over telephone lines.

module: a standard or basic unit for measuring; in the software sense, usually refers to a piece of a program that can be effectively handled as a single unit. Software engineers break large programming tasks into a set of modules that can be handled more efficiently.

monitoring system: the part of courseware that summarizes the information covered, the types of interactions the student made, and the results of any drills, quizzes, or tests managed by the software.

Murphy's Law: If anything can go wrong, it will go wrong.

network switch: the computer-based control center that routes long-distance telephone traffic.

node: a central connecting point in a communications network.

off-the-shelf software: a prepackaged or shrink-wrapped software product ready for use by the customer.

operating system: the software that controls the hardware and thus enables a computer to function. Creating it involves the most complex and demanding form of programming.

outsourcing: the practice of contracting the manufacture of a component to a third party in order to reduce costs.

parallel computers: a computer architecture that allows many operations to be performed simultaneously (that is, in parallel), thereby increasing the rate at which computations can be performed.

patching: a quick-and-dirty correction of an error in software, often done with little consideration of the side effects and typically poorly documented.

personal computer: a class of desktop machines that emerged in the early 1980s; they are inexpensive enough to be assigned to each person.

presentation system: the part of courseware responsible for delivering information to individual students.

process analyst: a software person who assesses the effectiveness of the software engineering process in an organization, taking measurements, soliciting opinions, and suggesting improvements.

production library: a computer-based storage facility where a business keeps its currently operating applications software.

product research group: the group in a software development organization responsible for monitoring the work of competing companies; also serves as a technology transfer agent, studying a new technology and defining local applications for it.

program: the set of instructions or codes a computer follows in order to perform a particular function.

programmer: a person who writes the instructions that constitute a computer program. In earlier years, that person also needed to understand the internal workings of a computer.

programming: the process of creating the sequences of instructions that allow a computer to function (also called coding).

programming language: a system of words and symbols that can be translated into elementary operations that can be performed by a computer; every language, such as COBOL, BASIC, and FORTRAN, has its own rules of grammar for conveying instructions.

prototype: a preliminary model of a product, often in graphic form, shown to customers in order to clarify their needs before the final product is built.

punched card: an obsolete card that records data in the form of combinations of holes made by a keypunch, and entered into a computer by a card reader.

quality analyst/engineer: a variation on the role of process analyst; a customer's in-house representative who is responsible for ensuring that good software engineering practices are being followed and high quality is being maintained. This person may work with software developers to help uncover problem areas and may perform quality assurance activities.

real-time process control: a real-time software system that monitors and operates some process, such as in a chemical plant.

real-time system: a combination of software and hardware that carries out its functions on a continuing basis and responds instantaneously to situations as they occur; for example, an avionics system of an aircraft is a real-time system.

resolution: a term used to describe the quality of computer graphics displays independent of the physical size of the display; often measured in dots per inch; a broadcast television picture has relatively low resolution, while a motion picture has very high resolution.

RISC: the acronym for reduced instruction set computer; refers to a computer architecture with a simplified set of instructions designed for solving special types of problems with maximum hardware speed from these simplified instructions.

shrink-wrapped software: a prepackaged software product for use on a personal computer. It is relatively inexpensive, is usually purchased through a retail outlet, and solves generic business or personal productivity problems, but it can also be tailored to a degree by its user.

soft job: a job in which people work with machines whose function (or what they produce) can change depending upon need.

soft key: a key on a terminal's keyboard whose function changes depending on what a user is doing and the context of the information being processed.

software: the information used to tap the potential of a computer; the programs or instructions that cause a computer to perform some function; the external manifestation of those programs seen by the computer user; the documents that describe how the programs work and how they are to be used; the data used by the programs as well as the data that are produced by them. Refers to both the actual product and the process encompassing people and the technology.

software-based system/product: any product or system that has software as a significant component; for example, a spreadsheet is a software product, while microwave ovens, cars, and modern cash registers are software-based products.

software crisis: a term coined in the 1960s to describe the inability of industry to meet the demand for software, particularly high-quality software.

software design: one aspect of a software engineer's job: defining the problem to be solved and creating a model for its solution.

software developer: a general term for anyone who creates and implements ideas in software.

software development: the entire process of designing, building, testing, and implementing software.

software engineer: a person who designs and builds software, has had formal training in software development, and uses specialized methods and tools. In earlier years, was referred to as a programmer.

software engineering: the process of designing and building software, using established requirements, standards, and procedures to produce a high-quality product.

software maintenance group: the group in a software development organization responsible for error correction, adaptations, and enhancements of software products.

software plant: part of any organization responsible for producing software.

software process: the sequence of events governing the creation of software.

software product: a set of computer programs that perform a particular function or satisfy a need; it is packaged in a form that can be supplied to end users.

software quality assurance group: the independent group in a software development organization that reviews and tests all software built and maintained within the company to assure it has high quality.

software shock: the stress and disorientation induced in individuals when software penetrates every aspect of their lives; includes the range of reactions, from fear to euphoria, toward interacting with and relying on software.

software tool: an entity that assists someone to perform a software-related task.

sorcerer: a software developer, or systems architect, who has outstanding technical skills and experience and who contributes to the software development organization both as a technician and as a teacher (also known as guru or wizard).

source code: the instructions in any programming language that make up a computer program; this human-readable text is translated into relatively arcane commands that are understood by the circuitry of a computer.

specification: a reference document containing the basic information that describes the details of needs, requirements, and functions for a new piece of software; it is usually one of the early steps in a software engineering process.

spreadsheet: a software product that allows end users to manipulate and analyze information (usually numbers) in rows and columns.

standards and procedures document: a collection or set of written guidelines to be followed in the software development process within an organization.

start-up company: a new company focused on one technology or product line characterized by a culture that is energetic, aggressive, and unconventional.

subcommittee paralysis: a situation resulting from too many subgroups working at cross purposes on aspects of a larger problem; usually results from their being excluded from the original committee formed to solve the problem.

systems management group: the group in a software development organization responsible for controlling the library of programs and documentation, handling the integration of the work done by the separate development and maintenance groups, packaging and shipping software releases, and cataloging and accounting for error reports produced by the customer support group. May also be responsible for computer operations, overseeing hardware repair, making backups, installing software updates, and generally policing all computer systems under its control.

systems software: the programs that control the use of computer resources and enable machines to perform their many functions.

technical manager: the manager responsible for organizing a project and coordinating the activities of the development team as well as of outsiders who work with the team.

top-down design/development: a method of software design and development that begins with establishing the overall requirements and architecture for the system. The role of the individual components is then defined in terms of the requirements and the architecture, and their design is made increasingly more detailed as design and development proceed.

turnkey software: a ready-to-use product (all the user must do is turn the key to use it); often tailored to the users' needs but tends to be expensive.

user: (*see* **end user**)

vector computers: computers introduced in the mid-1970s that can perform operations on many pieces of data simultaneously, thereby increasing the rate at which computations can be performed.

video conferencing: the technology that permits organizations to transmit both audio and video displays between locations in real time; it allows groups of people to conduct meetings without the need to be in the same room. Although currently expensive, it becomes attractive as travel and personnel costs increase.

videogram: a video presentation transmitted by and viewed on a computer screen.

virtual reality: (*see* **artificial reality**)

virus: a self-replicating, self-propagating program secretly embedded into another program or data file, that causes problems ranging from silly messages to malicious destruction of stored files (also known as worm).

voice mail: technology that permits a sender to store audio messages that can later be retrieved by the addressee.

the wall: an imaginary barrier that companies encounter because decision makers don't recognize the need for change, don't stay abreast of technology shifts, and stick to their old ways even when their competitors have abandoned similar approaches.

wizard: (*see* **sorcerer**)

workstation: a desktop computer with large computational capacity and high resolution graphics display. First designed for use by engineers but in recent years has moved into many other applications areas.

worm: (*see* **virus**)

young bull company: a start-up technical company that experiences rapid growth, focuses on one technology or product line, is very aggressive and confident, and maintains a high-pressured, goal-oriented environment.

Index

Other Titles Available
from Dorset House Publishing

Other Titles Available
from Dorset House Publishing

Peopleware
 by Tom DeMarco and Timothy Lister

Practical Project Management
 by Meilir Page-Jones

Productivity Sand Traps & Tar Pits
 by Mike Walsh

Quality Software Management: Volume 1, Systems Thinking
 by Gerald M. Weinberg

Rethinking Systems Analysis & Design
 by Gerald M. Weinberg

The Secrets of Consulting
 by Gerald M. Weinberg

Software Construction by Object-Oriented Pictures
 by George W. Cherry

Software Productivity
 by Harlan D. Mills

Software State-of-the-Art
 edited by Tom DeMarco and Timothy Lister

Strategies for Real-Time System Specification
 by Derek J. Hatley and Imtiaz A. Pirbhai

Understanding the Professional Programmer
 by Gerald M. Weinberg